Bridge To Success:

A Parent's Problem Prevention Guide

BY HENRY H WILLIAMSON JR

Copyright © 2014 Henry H Williamson Jr
All rights reserved.

ISBN: 1500760730
ISBN 13: 9781500760731

The Warm-up

To properly begin, let me say this: if you take nothing else from this book, take the idea that the most important thing you can do for you, your Little One, and the rest of us is to help him develop **self-discipline**. Keep in mind, for your child to develop self-discipline, *you must first impose discipline*, the key is, blanket it with **Love.**

Love is easy, **discipline** can be and usually is difficult, it must be practiced. Don't worry, we make it easy and fun as we guide you into the realm of *erecting* patterns of discipline. Those are the two essential items (discipline and love): sprinkle those with firm measures of **passion**; the result will be the undeniable position of a winner. Let me repeat that with emphasis: attention to **Love, Discipline,** and **Passion** are the undeniable *triplets of success*. The key is to integrate these themes into everything you do. Everything else: success and the ability to fully share the joys of life with your Little One will follow as a matter of course.

The secret to mastering and merging the triplets is important in the development of discipline. Here is where you enter the picture. Remember, we said, initially, the parent must first *impose* **discipline** upon his little "Bundle of Joy;" the goal is to *nudge* him into developing self-discipline. If the parent imposes this properly, self-discipline will develop quicker and with less complications and anguish than any method you select. That's easy to say, but how does a parent do it? Actually, it is also easy to do: just do **three big things**!

First, **talk often/listen intently** with your little "Bundle of Joy" as the object of your affection; initially, exactly what you say is not terribly

important. However, the important addition to words is your body language: provide **lots of hugs, kisses, and touches**. Now, here's another triplet: three things should accompany the words: smile, look the infant in the eyes as you speak, and seek acknowledgement from him: it might be goos, ahs, or just a smile; nevertheless, that makes it a two way proposition. (That's Logan and me in the bathtub)

However, there is another side to the "talk/listen saga," it is as important as anything you do as "leader of the pack." That is, listen, observe, and act on what your observations, and instincts reveal.

The responses from your Little One will aid in providing a path of open expression in later years. No need to say the words "I love you," but coupled with lots of hugs, kisses, and touches they say "I love you: 'I've got your back.'"

The second leg of the "big three things" is, be prepared to use the ingredients of "tough love" by issuing **lots of no's**. It is important to note that the parent should not overdo it; however, when you say "no," your little "Bundle of Joy" must **immediately** change his behavior. That should not be difficult; however, it can be because when you say "no," you must have a legitimate answer when the child says "Why not?"

More important than that is, there is almost always a question behind the question. "Ah ha! What's that?" Strange you should ask! The question behind the question is, "Who's in charge?" The answer behind the answer has to always be, "I am!" (the parent) Keep in mind, there is no need to boast or stick out your chest and declare "You da man," just make it subtle, matter of fact, that's the most effective manner to asserting your authority. When you use that approach, it can also be disarming to any challenges.

You might say, "This is getting complicated!" Not so, all you need to do is be **totally honest**! It is important that you don't bluff your way through any situation or question: if you know the answer to a question, that's great; on the other hand, if you have doubts or you don't know the answer; sometimes that might be even better. All you need to do is say, "I don't know, let's find out!" Then take him to the library, a dictionary, or a set of encyclopedias (it might be great if you have a set in your home: you be the judge.

The bottom line is, whenever your Little One asks a question; that time becomes a *teachable moment*. If you are on-course, there will be no need for you to reinforce the fact that you are in charge; however, if needed, teachable moments are the times to sport the fact that "You da man." Either way, teachable moments are precious: you'll have tons of them, try to recognize and take advantage whenever possible.

That idea highlights the fact that your responsibility as the parent is not to be your child's friend. You are the guide, protector, and molder of your little "Bundle of Joy:" that comes first. On the other hand, if you perform it properly, you will be the partner of a powerful individual and a life-long friend.

Now, here's where I place a wrinkle in your tinkle: whenever you say "No" to anyone, including your Little One (even though you are his hero), it causes the mind to begin to snap shut and could produce the beginning of rebellion. Your primary concern should be to avoid being placed in a position that interferes with the content of your (and especially his) "barrel of fun;" in other words (please don't hate me for this), in spite of what I said about "issuing lots of no's" (don't tighten up on me now), **almost never, ever say "No."**

There, I've said it!

"Issuing lots of "No's," and "almost never, ever say "No," sure seems like a contradiction doesn't it? Not so! There are two sides to the "No" saga. The side that says "no" is the black/white side; that could be used directly to support conditions involving safety, health, behavior, and a host of other issues. That's the tiny side. The other side is where you need to practice and become proficient with Parent's Alternate Phrases to "no," I call them the PAP's.

When you become proficient with using PAP's, not only will you become unstoppable in molding your Little One into that little stick of dynamite, you will also maintain that "barrel of fun" of which we speak. For example, your Little One might ask, "Daddy, can I cross the street without holding your hand?" You might say, "<u>No</u>!" (safety issue). On the other hand, you could develop a PAP like, "Can a cow see her ass?" (Oops, sorry about that, that was one of my dad's favorite expressions: I couldn't resist).

Anyhow, I think you get the idea.

On second thought, in case you don't get the idea, let me stretch it out for you. During the times you are having loads of fun, practice PAPs with your Little One via "no-games;" in other words, on occasion during a lull in play time, or any time for that matter, start a game of saying "no." The way it works: identify a known feature that you know your Little One knows the obvious answer; for example, "Is the fleece on Mary's little lamb green?" The answer: Mary had a little lamb, its fleece was white as snow! Or, "Jack and Jill went up the hill to fetch a pail of water!" The "no-game" might be, "Did Jack and Jill go up the hill to fetch a pail of ice cream?"

Ah ha, now you get the idea! Have fun with it as you develop your favorite PAPs.

Third of the big three things is, **limit giving foreign objects**: by foreign objects, I mean objects other than those that nature provides. If you refrain from giving your child too many toys, she will be more inclined to develop the inestimably important gift of imagination. I know that, if you can afford it, you probably will be tempted to provide generous numbers of toys. Give it some thought and consider this: experience has proven that children quickly lose interest in most toys. They are more intrigued with things that help them develop and exercise their imagination. Also keep in mind, the toys that your Little One leans toward the most will help you determine the nature of his life-long goals and desires (even when he might not be aware of them himself).

That's it for the "Three Big Things". See, that didn't take long, did it?

If you do them correctly, your Little One will begin to exhibit <u>self-discipline</u> at a much more consistent rate than otherwise. They are important because it causes your parent/child relationship to be much easier and much more fun. However, though the "big three things" are very important (it provides a non-threatening method of having fun with your Little One, at the same time instilling discipline), understanding and transferring the foundation of the **elements of the Factor of Five** is <u>essential</u>. Before we attack the core of this book we are going to tackle the **elements**, identify them as a package in a general context, wrap that package in a blanket of **discipline**, and use it as a foundation for the treatment of your "**Bridge to Success**."

Now, I'm going to start over again. I want to not waste your time; however, I do want to tie up a few loose ends and answer many questions you may have about our "Bridge to Success: A Parent's Problem Prevention Guide."

Bridge to Success

Hi, you have chosen to invest in a book that many have said**, "Finally, a practical book for parents."** Congratulations on a life-changing choice!

First of all, I want to thank you for choosing to read any part of this book. Obviously, you chose to view it because you thought it might be a source of enlightenment. You're correct, it is. However, this work was not written for the casual observer, the goal here is to mold lives: yours and your offspring.

Before we detail the exciting journey of this "Parent's Problem Prevention Guide," let me say**,** it is important to understand that everything (no exception) starts in the mind. **Your** mind has already been conditioned; in other words, you already have a foundation from which you are able to influence your little "Bundle of Joy." The magic of your relationship with your Little One is that he has a clean slate: his mind is like a CD that has already been formatted, it's just waiting to receive data.

The primary and overriding thing we are going to do is guide you into molding the waiting receptacle into a tower of joy, strength and power. What a marvelous tool you are, to be a catalyst in changing the world, just one individual at a time: your Little One.

The reason I call it a "problem prevention guide" is because of our manner of relating to your child, a ton of problems that many parents must solve, will never even raise their ugly heads. This "Bridge to

Success" guide will cause you, the parent, to fully enjoy and establish immersing yourself in a huge "barrel of fun".

You will be pleased to know you are going to be amazed at the results of our tutoring when your Little One is able to respond in such a manner that you fully understand the depth of his responses.

To properly begin, let me say this: if you take nothing else from this book, take the idea that the most important thing you can do for you, your Little One, and the rest of us is to help him develop **self-discipline**. Keep in mind, for your child to develop self-discipline, *you must first impose discipline*, the key is, blanket it with **Love.**

Love is easy, discipline can be and usually is difficult, it must be practiced (no worry, we guide you into the realm of erecting a pattern of discipline). Those are the two essential items: sprinkle those with firm benchmarks of **passion**: the result will be the undeniable position of a winner. Everything else, success and the ability to fully share the joys of life, will follow as a matter of course.

Some things that we seldom, if ever, think of, nevertheless are important; for example, a person's mindset. Have you ever thought about why the U.S.A. is so special? Well, I'll tell you. When the Founding Fathers of our great nation stepped away from Great Britain and announced a **Declaration of Independence**, the words were not just announcing a separation of powers, it was announcing the dawn of a new mindset.

The document began with the phrase, "We hold these truths to be self evident..." in other words, there is no doubt about the validity of the truth that "all men are created equal, that they are endowed by their Creator with certain unalienable Rights, that among these are Life, Liberty and the pursuit of Happiness..." Before that Declaration, no one had identified man's nature in just that way; the fact is, it changed the world.

That Declaration announced the dawn of a new mindset: the essence is stated, "I came, I saw, and I conquered the essence of life (not simply another nation)." When it comes to you and your Little One, I have identified that mindset and labeled it "the **Factor of Five.**" This is the formula we share with you for molding your child into a tower of strength and power.

The **Factor of Five** has two components. The first is the **Critical Three**, it involves the emotions of **LOVE** and **SEX**, plus the material symbolism that effects your emotions and your physical effort called **MONEY**. The remaining component involves the two factors that have a tendency to ooze into your Little One's mind and affect your success in a negative way. I call the potential negatives "the **Silent Spoiler**" and "**Family Relationships**."

Are you still with me? The reason I ask is that you are going to embark on a journey that will be exhilarating and magical, and you'll see the results of your effort develop each and every day, minute, hour, second via your little "Bundle of Joy".

That's exciting.

Even before we start our engines, allow me a pause to allow you to relax and enjoy your anticipated involvement. Again, another tidbit we seldom, if ever think about. I offer you just a brief comment about the symbols that represent us to the world. First is the flag of the U.S.A., the other is the dollar sign (the symbol of our currency): I know it's rather difficult to relate a symbol to an infant, he has no idea of the concept or meaning; however, by your actions you can guide him toward recognizing and implementing the forces that make the flag and money relevant. Just as the **Star Spangled Banner** (our national flag) is a symbol, so is **the dollar**. Both of them represent the same thing: the power of individual achievement, they are both moved by emotion (Love and Sex), and production (Money).

Here is simply an exercise to highlight the value of symbols: superimpose the letter "U" (United) on top of the letter "S," (States), placed together, the result is the symbol for our currency. When we pledge allegiance to our flag, that act is not just a detached statement of patriotism. It is a **declaration of independence**: independent thought, independent assessment of liberty and justice for all. The fact is, it is in everyone's best interest to keep the above in mind as you communicate the meaning and symbols to your Little One. That's what a salute, and/or placing your hand over your heart during the playing of our national anthem is all about. I think that's significant.

Now, let's get on with it!

When it comes to the parent/child relationship, especially during the formative years, everything we do and in all areas of life: our joys, sorrows, and successes are related to just three things: **Love**, **Sex**, and **Money** – I call them the primary elements of the **Factor of Five**.

We'll talk more about that very shortly; meanwhile, I'm excited! You'll be excited too when you look at your Little One and see what you and he/she have accomplished after you have followed the guidelines within this book.

Careful now, before you continue, I want you to know this book is about changing society – one individual at a time. You and others like you and I, are the individuals. The good news is, with the aid and guidelines outlined here, you will be better able to mold your Little One into a tower of strength and power.

Incidentally, before this book was published, a Bridge to Success website was established. http://www.bridge2successdesign.com, tens of thousands of individuals and families have acknowledged the effectiveness of the simple yet heartwarming methods, technique, or whatever you prefer to call them resident within the covers of this book! Actually, your success depends upon your ability to relate your mindset to your little "Bundle of Joy." There are a few keys that you, the parent, will want to embrace: the first is to personalize the guide to fit your unique parent/child relationship. In other words, make it your blueprint to success!

Again! Welcome and thanks in advance for helping change our society into the way you want it to be.

One more thing: if you are male or female, wealthy or homeless, black or white, fat or thin, immigrant or natural born, Christian or atheist, "gay" or "straight" (did I miss anybody? Oh yes: elderly and/or youthful!), the methodology is equally effective. Again, thank you for opening your mind to your Little One's "Bridge to Success."

Even as I say it, I know you might be thinking, "What an outrageous statement: the man must be full of grandeur and egotism!" Many others may possess similar thoughts. My response is, none of that is accurate; however, "The proof of the pudding is in the eating." In other words, continue reading: follow the guide, if at any point you find the reasoning is faulty, or the goals are insecure or insincere, or it is obvious that a particular idea simply will not work – stop! Put the book down and keep it to yourself.

I'm just kidding: but, if you really believe this book is not worthy of your attention, return it, tell me why (send an email to, parentchild4now@gmail.com, Subject line: "Disappointed"), and I'll send you a gift plus reimburse you for your effort.

On the other hand, if you find this book really does what I say: "change lives: yours and your offspring," then the best thing you can do is share the contents with as many other parents as you possibly can. Keep in mind, it's not the book, it is not the writer – it is <u>you</u> who will cause change in your life and the lives of others. This book is simply the catalyst, and most certainly should be shared with other parents; in fact, it should be shared with everyone, parent or not.

Maybe you're thinking, "Those sure are fancy words, but words without action are as fruitful as a good looking apple that has a worm inside." If that is what you're thinking, you are absolutely correct, and your concerns are worthy of attention. With that in mind, let me tell you, and lead you to the "Bridge to Success" that will cause a change in you, and at the same time caress the level of your current core of success.

To obtain a better sense of the content and value of this work, please allow me to share the secret of why the change in you will occur; actually, it's not a secret at all; it's a formula, and it has two components: simplicity and ownership. It is uncomplicated: it tackles the two parts that make us who we are: the body and the mind (soul). The other part is, it establishes an all-encompassing technique of ownership, and is made easy by aiding you in personalizing the interrelationship between you and your child.

This book was not written to change your offspring, rather to mold him to be the best individual possible, and to enjoy every minute of the journey toward independence. The best thing to be said about the content of this effort is, the method of integration is simple and easy to personalize; in fact, that's one of the permanent keys: personalizing the technique. Make it **your** unique roadmap!

Having said that, it is important to keep in mind that this book is not about me, it's not about you, or the government or politics. It is a book that will aid you in building and molding your child from infancy to adulthood; here, we are concerned with the foundation of your child. That foundation is sculptured during the first five to seven years of your Little One's life: in our case, we take it from birth to five years. The result will be an individual who will be strong, forthright, honest, and a credit to himself and humanity.

Before I continue, let me attempt to release myself from possible misunderstanding about the title I chose. What I mean by that is, "success" and "prevention" in the same sentence may cause a person to be undecided about selecting this book. Well, there is no need to waver because I understand that I am special; however, I also understand that I am no more special than you. The fact is, our Creator provided each of us with everything we need, to be all we desire. What that means is, it's not who or what we are, it's how we utilize our assets: the secret is to identify <u>specifically</u> what we want (our goals), then <u>focus</u> on the details.

The next thing is to answer the question that you probably are asking: "How does this man qualify to talk about parenting?" Good question. There is more than just one answer, let me start with the primary one: I am a parent, and have been for more than four decades. Once a parent, always a parent: that means nothing, it's just a fact. However, I said that to say that everyone has two parents, yet not everyone can be a parent.

I was born in December 1938, and became a parent for the first of three times in July, 1971. The first was a girl, the other two were boys: born 1980 and 1984. The dates and gender are important because a parent never knows the quality of his effort until he/she looks at the offspring after entry in adulthood. For the most part, the individuals who can best answer that question are grandparents or the equivalent.

Another reason I qualify is that prominent in the results you'll achieve is a matter that went undetected by me for many years. In fact, ten years ago, had someone asked me if I thought I had been a good parent, I would have answered "Yes, absolutely!"

Wrong! I discovered just a few short years ago that I had been a lousy parent. The realization caused me to observe successful parenting from the standpoint of a parent/child relationship. After my research, including observation of successful parents, I realized the result of successful/good parenting is when, prior to the child reaching independent adulthood, he has a core belief that will help survive the ravages of change.

In other words, when the child has reached adulthood, if he feels good about himself, relates well to others, and is a productive individual (regardless of financial position), then you have done it: your "child" is living proof! The book you hold in your hands is the result of positive actions based upon successful-parenting observations and action.

Very shortly, I'm going to identify the value of: **Three Big Things**. Those two terms (the **Factor of Five** and **Three Big Things**) comprise the essence of the Bridge to Success. Remember, we said one of the things that makes this work so extraordinary is the result of two things: simplicity and ownership. It is also the result of treating the life of you and your Little One, the way the Creator intended. In other words Life is a "barrel of fun".

What does all that mean? It means, you're going to enjoy being yourself, being a parent, and molding a human being into a little stick of dynamite: a tower of power. Just one little tidbit: ultimately your material wealth is not terribly important (Penthouse or street-dweller), the key to success with your child is to build a relationship of trust by being totally honest and giving of your insides, and by using your mindset to mold him to be all he is meant to be. This book is designed to aid you in accomplishing that goal.

I may not be... let me rephrase that... I am not the brightest tool in the shed, but I do know that short of keeping our child cut off from the world in a bubble, we have only a small influence on him. Some parents choose home schooling to detour around that problem; however, for the most part we know our children will spend a good part of their time under the influence of authority figures other than you, the parent. Oftentimes, we don't even know very much about the authority figures filling our children's heads with ideas.

In the past, many families lived in close communities where if a child acted in a manner that you wouldn't approve, another parent would think nothing of exerting appropriate disciplinary measures, then sending him home. In addition, children spent much more time with an extended family; plus, the churches and synagogues played a much more important role in the culture and seasons of life.

If you think about the time your child is not within your purview, you can see your influence lessening. Add to that the influence of television, with hundreds of channels: the internet, video games, and other distractions, you can see why parents might need to be extra vigilant or downright overprotective. With that in mind, I think you can agree, we can all see societal chaos. In other words, we can all see our younger generations moving further away from visions we want for our children's future, as well as the future of humanity. Having said that, many of us believe, the only thing we can control is what we do right now.

With that in mind, I believe the most effective way we can reverse the deteriorating trend in which our society is headed, is to begin at the beginning. We do that by being aware of what's happening now and by taking simple yet orchestrated steps to transform the destination.

We know the source of strength and weakness in any society is the degree of freedom individuals possess to be what they were created to be. That is also one of the things that make mankind unique and you, the parent, so important.

We also know, change does not begin with a writer, or a book, nor does it begin with any government or governmental agency. It begins with you. Each of us can sit back, and by default, allow someone else to determine our fate and the fate of our little "Bundle of Joy," or we can take charge and build a new society, one safe and secure child at a time. Whichever the case, it starts with <u>you</u>.

However, long before your Little One understands words, he gathers generalized impressions about himself and the new world around him. Whether you are a mom or dad, you should know basic information about him that will cause your parenting adventure to be easier or tougher.

Regardless of the nature of his birth, he is sensitive to whether he is lifted tenderly or jerked around like a sack of potatoes: he senses that the arms around him are warmly close or give only vague disinterested support. The touch, body movements, muscle tensions, tones and facial expressions that you present, sends him an ongoing message: his sensitivity is amazingly accurate.

Believe me: it makes a big difference if you focus on your Little One rather than the task to be done; for example, when he is bathed you want to have your muscles relaxed, your tone playful and soft, and you want to have a gentle light in your eyes that says, "You are a valued asset: I love you!"

In addition, you want to visualize his little fat wrinkles and dimpled toes as simply part of a delightful adventure in his reactions to the water you drip on his little belly-button. When he gurgles from the joy he experiences from knowing he is alive in his new world, and he splashes his fists in the water, he sees your laughing reaction as you joining in his game. That's his and your blended mindset at work! It's called bonding!

At that point, no words can be or need be spoken, but the two of you will be communicating within the earliest stages of bonding. He will feel and see your responsiveness, and even though he is now a separate entity, he will sense the early experience of being valued. That is extremely important, it will make his experience and yours much easier in the transformation from fetus to child.

Just as an aside, while I was at the YMCA a few days ago, I observed a woman sitting in a chair near me. She used her Little One's bottle-time as an opportunity for reading a book. She didn't even hold him, her attention was not on him, it was on her book. When he cooed, she ignored his sound. When he moved about, she was unresponsive. She and her Little One were not sharing an experience; in fact, there was no warm, human, direct person-to-person encounter at all. Apparently, the caretaker was not aware that she was his whole world at that time in space: those first experiences could be teaching him the world is a cold, heartless place in which he has little or no importance.

If she was the mother, she will pay a price for her indifference; on the other hand, maybe she was a baby sitter, whatever the case, all is not lost. Experiments with infants suggest the degree of warm responsiveness provided by parents, provide the foundation for a future elevated view of his identity. We'll talk about the importance of identify later.

Sorry for the lengthy aside, I just thought it might be a significant observation. Let's continue.

The responsiveness we highlight within the covers of this book is made up of **three big things** (things that support and reflect warm respect and delight with your Little One), it blankets the **factor of five**. The reflections we refer to in each instance support your Little One in getting started toward self-identity.

At this point, I want to attend to a minor, but possibly confusing incidental – terminology: in search of uniform and flowing consistency, I will limit the use of gender (him/her -- he/she, etc.). You have probably already observed, I use he or him almost exclusively. To get around that, if your Little One is female, think pink, if male think blue. Hopefully, my female friends (don't you simply love them) will not take offense. Having said that, let's continue.

Now, where do we go from here? Experts who seem to know about success say people learn more from failure than from success. Well, I say "Hang on, 'cause if that's true (I believe it is) you are in for quite a ride."

Problem Prevention (Overview)

Select anything a person wants to do or be, and there is a book out there that will help guide him to achieve his objective. In this case, there are tons of books related to parenting that are worthy of attention and that are much more in depth than this one. They cover pregnancy, childcare, discipline, behavior, medical problems, games, and on and on. In fact, some are so good that I have read and listed many of them in my limited bibliography of reference.

Having said that, I want to make it clear that the intent here is not to take away from any positive efforts by anyone, it's just to add to them. This effort differs from the others because we tackle the foundation of our being in a manner that leads to the culmination of a person who faces life with passion, anticipates joyful noises of success, and leads himself and all who associate with him to the realization of worthy goals. Meanwhile, please, pretty please, don't make a big deal of it; on the other hand, it is a big deal. I am referring to the importance of the act of goal setting, planning, and working the plan. Think about it, but let's not dwell on it too deeply.

Fact: every child is different, and every parent is different in relation to each child, even if the child is a twin or any other multiple. Nevertheless, there are five consistent stages and levels each parent/child will encounter. Although the stages are etched in stone, the ages will vary somewhat, they are:

Stage	Age	Level of Parenting Activity
1	0 – 1	Love, discipline, molding, teaching, learning
2	1 – 5	Reinforcing the mold
3	5 – 7	Countering outside influences
4	7 – 13	Guiding/directing toward life-long occupation
5	13 – 21	Reinforcing and supporting the child's focus and direction.

I was a masterful parent during stage one and two with my daughter and older son, but a bust with each of them during all the other stages. There were legitimate reasons, primarily resulting from stupidity. If I were to highlight any one or all the reasons, that would be a continuation of the stupid label. With that in mind, I think you will agree, there is no need to linger on that fact. One thing that might cause you to want to continue reading this book is that experts insist that individuals learn more from failure than from success. I believe that's true, which means you are in for quite a ride.

I think I said that before? No matter, it is no less true!

If comments from readers of the manuscript, and those who accessed my "Bridge to Success" website, "http://www.bridge2successdesign.com," are any indication, you just hang on: you and your Little One will gain immense value, and because of that, so will your community.

I said it before and I'll say it again: just as there are two components to being a human being, there are two components to being a parent.

The first and most important is the parent's mindset. It is the major issue of being a "good/successful parent." The major emphasis of this work is devoted to that issue. It is of utmost importance because the behavior of your Little One stems from the mental outlook that you create and mold. That's the essence of part one: our goal is to aid you in providing a successful mindset for your little "Bundle of Joy".

The second component is what you do. Everything, without exception, begins in the mind; however, nothing happens until we transfer our thoughts into action. That's where the parent(s) helps develop the physical skills that make it easy and fun for your Little One to, slowly but surely, show how he is in control of his worldly existence. (That's my younger son, Troy, during the time he was determined to be the greatest detective in the world!)

That is the essence of part two of our Bridge to Success. I hope you agree that we have set the foundation for the beginning of our journey, thank you for having an open mind about being a "good/successful parent."

Now, let's take a brief look at the table of contents: it's a short book, but it is packed with power. I know, I know, that's what I say. Well, tens of thousands of others agree with me; give it a shot, I truly believe, so will you.

After you view the contents, I'll be back for a brief comment about "Humilipride" and respect. Then off to the races!

Table of Contents

The Warm-up · iii
Bridge to Success · ix
Problem Prevention (Overview) ·xix
Foreword · xxv

PART ONE · 1
Chapter One   Is there a Doctor in the house? · · · · · · · · · · · · · 3
Chapter Two   Three Big Things · 9
Chapter Three   The Critical Three · 15
Chapter Four   The Silent Spoiler · 45
Chapter Five   RAM Time · 53
                               Spiritual Aid · 61
                               Power of the Parent! · · · · · · · · · · · · · · · · · · 67
Appendix A   Checklist of Progress · · · · · · · · · · · · · · · · · · 77
Appendix B   What to do to guide your little one to… · · · · · · · · 83

PART TWO · 85

SECTION ONE · 89
Chapter One   From Birth to Six Months · · · · · · · · · · · · · · · · 91
Chapter Two   From Six Months to One Year · · · · · · · · · · · · 103

SECTION TWO	THE FINAL FOUR	115
Chapter One	(From One to Two Years)	117
Chapter Two	From Two to Three Years	123
Chapter Three	From Three to Four Years	127
Chapter Four	From Four to Five Years	131
Chapter Five	From Home to School	135
Bibliography		139
Appendix C	Nursery Rhymes	141
Appendix D*	Typical Course of Study (before computer input)	143
Appendix E	How to Control an Object	147
	How to Throw a Ball (any object)	151
	How to catch a ball (any object)	155
	Games (Variations) (Physical/Mental)	161
Appendix F	Acknowledgement	163

Foreword

I'm so excited to get on with it, I could shout, but I won't, I just want to reveal what you're in store for before I really get going. So if you'll bear with me just a little longer, I'm certain you'll appreciate the delay.

Rearing children has been the most exciting adventure in the lives of untold numbers of men and women <u>and</u> the most important. On the other hand, it usually is not the easiest. Regardless of how one says it, all parents have dreams for their children, and RIGHT NOW is the time to begin making those dreams come true. The question is; how does one begin? Some enlightened enthusiasts say one answer is, <u>read this book,</u> then follow up on the content!

Our number one job as parents is to nudge our joyful infants in such a way that they arrive as adults in a position to totally enjoy the best that life has to offer. The eye-opening reality is that it does not have to be attached to their financial position.

Many parents miss the boat in instilling the proper mindset that will help propel their Little One's to heights of genuine self-reliance, self-importance, and the reality of expecting and accepting consequences in all they do. They do that by thinking in terms of the dollar. No problem; however, with the proper mindset, the dollar will take care of itself.

Later in the life of your Little One, he may need to introduce a reality check such as needing a day-job to support his intended occupation. Or of obtaining an education; however, we are not at that stage, we are working on the foundation. We know with the proper mindset, children will grow naturally into their talent and desires.

Also, many adult Americans are stalled from catching the train to happiness by not fully realizing that the life of a human being is complex. On the other hand, with proper guidance, the understanding of life's challenges can take on the appearance of being "no big deal." By identifying and conquering the elements of the **Factor of Five**, parents will provide the mental tools to secure a foundation for their Little One relating to self worth, sexual concerns, and financial stability. Each of these areas is easy to conquer if we start at the beginning. That's where this book comes in – at the beginning.

One more thing before we attack this project: I want to be careful to note that the desire to influence the progress of your new arrival, regardless of the level of his ability to learn, is essential to his development. It is the belief of many who have read this book, and/or visited my website, http://www.bridge2successdesign.com, that the approach outlined within these pages will enhance and improve every parent/child relationship, and tackle patterns leading to learning efficiency (Movigenics).

Having said that, there is a point to be made here that could impact the successful interrelationship and subsequent joyful production of all that is relevant in the life of your Little One. It's a tough one because handled **improperly**; it could cause setbacks in his development. With this book as your guide, your Little One will tend to advance very quickly and enjoy every minute of his progress and achievement; however, achievement produces pride and pride can very well produce arrogance. That's a problem we want to avoid because it can cause the way others relate to and embrace his achievements.

Never, ever intentionally rain on his parade. The fact is, regardless of how well and how quickly he matures, there are other individuals existing under the same conditions that will do better, in some instances, much better than your Little One. He should be made aware of that fact, but in simple and subtle ways. In other words, help develop a trait in him I call "humilipride". Humilipride is the position one attains where he is proud of his achievements and acknowledges that he is special; at the same time, understands that his success is a normal human trait. The result is that humility will tend to cradle his achievements.

Since your lifetime goal for him is to achieve maturity and independence, one way to show humility is to assume his elders have already achieved that standard. He can respectfully honor their achievement by conferring on them the title of "Sir/Ma'am." Some individuals might say, "That's sweet, but no need to be formal with me, young man, you can just call me Sue." Your Little One can then answer, "Thank you Ma'am… I mean Sue."

You might say, "What's the big deal?" There is no big deal, the point here is, don't get caught up with the small stuff: the idea is simply to treat everyone with **respect** (that could be important to them), it could make a difference in their support of his image (that could be important to your Little One).

The above can be a tricky one, don't overdo it: just be aware of it. Don't you just love the way life is a challenge, and that because of our nature, we can make joyful noises to all the land and praise the goodness it offers.

Now, let's get started…I know, I know, I said that before. I guess the reason I might appear to say things over and over is that this book is designed to be absorbed in segments. I could say, "I'm only human," but I cringe when people say that, we are at the top of the food-chain, so get over it! Ughhh, that sounded harsh didn't it, sorry about that.

PART ONE

CHAPTER ONE

Is there a Doctor in the house?

Ancient Indian Proverb: *"Treat the earth well: it was not given to you by your parents, it was loaned to you by your children. We do not inherit the Earth from our ancestors; we borrow it from our children."* I admit, that sounds backwards; however, you might want to reflect on that Proverb, meanwhile...

This book is designed to aid parents in molding their children in forming a solid foundation of strength and power. Many parents have been heard to say, "Wouldn't it be great if there were a book on parenting? It sure would be nice!" Well, here you have it: this is a guide that will aid you in molding a child to be all the Creator intended him to be. The time span involves the most critical span of time in your child's life: from birth to five years of age. That time-span is when you set the foundation for all challenges your child will endure. The wonderful and magical thing is by personalizing the guidelines in this book, you will be part of the Bridge to Success. In other words, you and your Little One will enjoy life as it is meant to be: a "barrel of fun!"

In the past, parents were confused and disappointed when their children misbehaved. The Bible says "Spare the rod, spoil the child," that might mean, inflict pain on the child to correct unacceptable behavior, especially when the child embarrasses his parent(s). The only problem with that is parents will sometimes become angry and turn the spanking into a beating, sometimes to the degree that it results in child abuse. They call it "corporal punishment". Well, let's talk about that. What is "corporal punishment?"

The dictionary defines **Corporal punishment** as a form of impact on a child that involves the deliberate infliction of pain as retribution for an offense, or for the purpose of disciplining or reforming a wrongdoer, or to deter attitudes or behavior deemed unacceptable. The term usually refers to methodically striking the offender with the open hand or with an implement, whether in judicial, domestic, or educational settings. Incidentally, I used to hate it when my mom instructed me to "go get me a switch," I knew what was coming next!

Corporal punishment is defined by the UN Committee on the *Rights of the Child* as: "any punishment in which physical force is used and intended to cause some degree of pain or discomfort, however light." Incidentally, children have the same RIGHTS as the rest of us: Life, Liberty, and the pursuit of Happiness. For example, a child has the RIGHT to be rude, obstructive, and abrasive; on the other hand, the parent(s) has the RIGHT to apply consequences. This is the time to define a RIGHT: a RIGHT exists only if it does not require someone else to make it happen.

In spite of that definition by the esteemed world body, "corporal punishment" of minors within domestic settings is still lawful in 49 of the 50 United States. Only the tiny state of Delaware outlawed it as "child abuse" (they did that in 2012).

Incidentally, In the year 2000, the result of a survey involving "Corporal Punishment," determined it was widely approved by U.S. parents. ^ Reaves, Jessica. "Survey Gives Children Something to Cry About", *Time*, New York, 5 October 2000.

Nevertheless, if you think "corporal punishment" is cruel and unusual, and that the parents who practice it are mean and inhumane, you might be correct; on the other hand, you are a prime candidate to be a lousy parent.

If you think "corporal punishment" is needed to keep children in line, and lack of it is the reason we have such a problem with our kids today; then you might need to re-think your requirements of what is needed to keep "children in line".

In my day, Dr. Spock was the end-all of parental advice. If you think he spoiled a complete generation because many parents believed he knew more about parenting than they did (after all, he was a Doctor), then personalizing the guidelines in this book is probably your "cup of tea".

If you have been looking for a practical book that will cause "corporal punishment" to be unnecessary, will provide the necessary ammunition to provide the parenting skills a caring parent needs, will address and counteract theories such as those proposed by Dr. Spock, then continue reading this book.

In fact, "corporal punishment" is a misconception of how to correct aberrant behavior. That's one reason corporal persuasion: not "corporal punishment" (when used judiciously) might be effective; on the other hand, when used in excess or as a means of punishment, it can be detrimental to your relationship with your Little One.

You may disagree, but I guarantee you, there is <u>never</u> a need to **punish** your child (strong, but true statement). The reason is your Little One is the result of your input; in other words, because of your input or lack of it (by default) he is exactly the way you have taught him to be. In still other words, if punishment is to be inflicted, you should be the one to be punished.

That's a contentious statement, I know, I simply said it to support, "never a need to punish your child." However, when the need arises, your responsibility in molding him to expect to be accountable for his actions, might be to activate painful consequences.

Caution: a spanking should be very brief; it is intended to provoke tears and pain, but no harm. A beating is different: it is defined as extended, harmful, painful behavior by a more physically, more powerful individual. The point is, beating your child provides no beneficial results and it should be forbidden (by you), mainly because it provides limited aid in molding your child or changing his inappropriate behavior. On the other hand, it might cause him to be resentful and seek vengeance ("whenever he can weasel out an opportunity"). A parent may be disappointed with a child's behavior; sure, it can cause the beginnings of anger, but never strike a child in anger, and never strike him in the face.

Now, pay attention! (I know I shouldn't say it quite that way, but this is an extra important point): when the need to activate painful consequences arises, you should look your child in the eyes, and an explanation of the cause of the event should be exchanged with him. The major key is that it should be completed immediately after the act (in some instances "immediate" might be after the two of you arrive back at home). The attached structure is that it should be completed in such a way as to elicit acknowledgement from him that he understands your action and the need for invoking painful consequences.

That interchange will do at least three things: it will reduce the need to invoke painful consequences in the future, it will reduce ill-will with him (especially if the delay in immediacy is to avoid embarrassing him), and it will cause a ripple effect (a tradition of parental activity); what I mean by that is, when he becomes a parent, he will be inclined to say to <u>his</u> Little One, "Here are the consequences of your action, and this is the reason why. You do understand that, right?" (that should be stated in your own words). One or two good, solid swats on the back of the hand, followed by a hug, will usually be adequate. On the other hand, an extended "spanking" (not beating) might be necessary if he continues to be obstinate (you be the judge).

In addition, the interchange technique insures (to a degree, to both you and your Little One) that the spanking is necessary. You don't have to be there to know that following up with that technique (including a sincere hug) can be magical!

If you are a parent, or your children are preparing to become parents, there is no better guide to erecting a "Bridge to Success", than cuddling with this book. If you are a grandparent, you are fully aware of the result of your efforts as a parent. When you read this book, you will know beyond a shadow of doubt that this is a substantial guidepost for every parent, especially the new one. The reward is that you will enjoy your grandchildren to an even greater extent.

Sometimes we don't think about the idea that everyone has two parents; however, not everyone will be, want to be, or can be, a parent. However, if you find yourself in the position of caregiver, you will find the object of this book is to provide you with essential tools needed to bridge the gap between infancy and adulthood -- that is not a simple task. The primary reason for that is, we humans need a solid foundation to survive the trauma of changing conditions. In the case of individuals (I said it before), the foundation is erected during the first five to seven years of his existence (think pink/blue – wasn't that easy?).

The five-year timeframe is the focus of this book because it encompasses the span prior to the school systems corrupting your little "Bundle of Joy." By reading and absorbing the essentials within these pages, both the parent and child can expect to experience life as it is meant to be: a "barrel of fun" and excitement. Many of you may be thinking, "What does he mean, 'prior to the school systems corrupting (my) child.'"

That's an excellent question, let me be clear about that: we have an abundance of teachers who provide our youth with unique methods to solve a variety of problems: each of us should be grateful for their positive contribution. On the other hand, our teachers should be gearing our youth toward the foundation with the thought in mind to better determine truth from fiction (an individual does that by adhering to the fact that the core of truth is consistency along with brevity). In addition, teachers should be partnering with parents in an effort toward maintaining a moral compass supporting the idea that life is a "barrel of fun".

To continue: Without the help of others (not the government), no one can accomplish anything worthwhile: all of us need help. There were many, many others who aided in the success of this effort. With that thought in mind, allow me to add a point of acknowledgement for part one of this work. Especially valuable was the input by ... oooooh, I almost dropped the ball. I was about to thank and acknowledge the special input by certain parents, but that would delay getting started with the focus of this effort. So, phooey on that!

On the other hand, I am extremely grateful to those who, by their parenting skills, are responsible for much of the contents within this effort. In addition to my Grandpa and grandma, there are five parents and their spouses whom I'd like to acknowledge because they have proven the value of good/successful parenting [they compose the Board of Successful Parenting (BOSP)]. That acknowledgement appears in Appendix F.

One final item before we begin: many individuals have found that one of the primary methods of achieving success at anything we do is to find someone who is already successful at whatever it is; find out what he did and mimic him. However, because of the fact that every parent is different and every child is different in relation to the parent, mimicry may not always produce parent/child success. That's one of the things that causes this book to be unique. The techniques/methods outlined here enhance both the sameness and differences in the parent/child relationship. In other words, you'll know when and how to mimic, and when and how to lead the charge to a new frontier of joyful interaction with your Little One.

Now, "let's begin our project, or as the wrestling guy likes to say, "Let's get ready to rumbleee!"

CHAPTER TWO

Three Big Things

The **Factor of Five** identifies everything we do and in all areas of life: our joys, sorrows, and successes are related to just three things: <u>Love</u>, Sex, and Money – Those are the major elements.

Mastering and understanding those elements will tend to free the parent's and child's hearts from hatred. It will also make unnecessary mental anguish about things one cannot change. In addition, it will cause a person to live simply, give more, and expect less. And here is the decisive difference-maker: since the real source of happiness is not material belongings, it will produce awareness that real wealth is the resident of contents <u>inside</u> a person (the core of an individual), not outside (physical appearance). However, also keep in mind, success leaves clues; in other words, a person's physical appearance might be an indication that uncovers the core of his being.

The secret to mastering the **"Factor of Five"** is important in the development of <u>discipline</u>. Here is where you enter the picture. Remember, we said, initially, the parent must first ***impose* discipline** upon his little "Bundle of Joy;" the goal is to *nudge* him into developing <u>self-discipline</u>. If the parent imposes this properly, self-discipline will develop quicker and with less complications and anguish than any other method. That's easy to say, but how does a parent do it? Actually, it is also easy to do: just do **three big things**!

First, **<u>talk often/listen intently</u>** with your little "Bundle of Joy" as the object of your affection; in addition, provide **<u>lots of hugs, kisses, and touches</u>**; initially, exactly what you say is not terribly important.

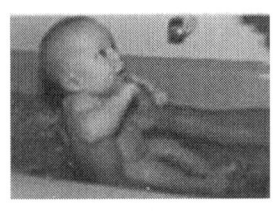

However, three things should accompany the words: smile, look the infant in the eyes as you speak, and seek acknowledgement from him: it might be goos, ahs, or just a smile; nevertheless, that makes it a two way proposition. (That's Logan and me in the bathtub)

However, there is another side to the "talk/listen saga," it is as important as anything you do as "leader of the pack." That is, listen, observe, and act on what your observations, and instincts (your gut reaction) reveal.

Those words (responses) will aid in providing a path of open expression in later years. No need to say the words "I love you," but coupled with lots of hugs, kisses, and touches they say "I love you: 'I've got your back.'"

On the other hand, too many hugs, kisses, and touches may be counter-productive. With that in mind the caregiver needs a key that will help advance him to the forward direction. Here it is, I call it the "**Smile Index** (SI)." When your Little One stops smiling, you know you are approaching the wrong direction. When that happens, you might want to stop everything and change direction: your gut instinct will direct you. Keep in mind, very few things are carved in stone; however, when the child smiles, it tells you he is feeling security and love. In addition, that feeling provides the opening stage toward independent associations.

Before we advance to the second leg of the "three big things," one thing is vital and beyond dispute: your Little One is extremely observant. He sees everything around him because to him everything is "new". Keep in mind that what you say must be consistent with what you do and how you do it, otherwise he will be confused and his progress will be slowed. For example, if you engage in activities with one or more significant other(s) -- husband/wife, boy/girl friend -- the treatment of her or him should be consistent with the treatment of your Little One.

That's not to say hugs and kisses should or should not be part of that relationship; however, touching is the foundation of caring: there should be lots of touching (but not too much, just be careful). The handshake is a prime example, even when a person is not known to you, a handshake is an excellent opening. That seems elemental; however, it is very important because to achieve optimum progress from your Little One, he should perceive that life is a "barrel of fun". A handshake or equivalent tends to caress the "barrel of fun".

One more thing, let's just pause and pay strict attention to a phrase we used just a minute ago, "Your Little One is extremely observant." That means he sees your strengths **and** your weaknesses (all of them!). "Uh, uh! Really?" Yep really. But don't let that bother you, you can work on your weaknesses and strengthen your strong suit; nevertheless, whatever you do, even if you don't work on your strengths/weaknesses, "make it happen and make it fun!" (it's just that the weaker you are, the tougher it will be to assert your success-agenda). The key is to be consistent; in other words, let your action (what you do) agree with your words (what you say).

The second leg of the "big three things:" be prepared to use the ingredients of "tough love" by issuing **lots of no's**. It is important to note that the parent should not overdo it; however, when you say "no," your little "Bundle of Joy" must **immediately** change his behavior. That should not be difficult; however, it can be because when you say "no," you must have a legitimate answer when the child says "Why not?"

Keep in mind that you hope he feels confident enough in your "no" response to accept it without question. On the other hand, you also want him to be open and confident enough in you to ask, **on occasion**, "Why not." Also keep in mind that "Because I said so" is not a legitimate answer. Nevertheless, if you believe or **feel** that "no" is the correct response to a situation or question, to say "no" is better than to say "yes." One more thing: sometimes it's in the best interest of both of you to provide a legitimate reason for your "no-response" no later than the next encounter. On the other hand, to just let it lay is usually the best (the same or similar situation will probably raise its head many times).

You might say, "What's the big deal?" The "big deal" is, if you can't provide a legitimate answer to your child's inquiry, the control of him might take a sizable hit, plus it is guaranteed he will test you again in short order. It might be about something different, but the test is sure to come: your response might be crucial. Regardless of outcome, remember: the "no" idea is to set the foundation for the development of ***self- discipline***.

More important than that is, there is almost always a question behind the question. "Ah ha! What's that?" Strange you should ask! The question behind the question is, "Who's in charge?" The answer behind the answer has to always be, "I am!" (the parent) Keep in mind, there is no need to boast or stick out your chest and declare "You da man," just make it subtle, matter of fact, that's the most effective manner to asserting your authority (when you use that approach, it can also be disarming to your potential adversaries).

Incidentally, I'll say it one more time: the parent might be female: the reason I use the masculine terminology is because it keeps the flow uniform.

You might say, "This is getting complicated!" Not so, all you need to do is be totally honest! It is important that you don't bluff your way through any situation or question: if you know the answer to a question, that's great; on the other hand, if you have doubts or you don't know the answer; sometimes that might be even better. All you need to do is say, "I don't know, let's find out!" Then take him to the library, a dictionary, or a set of encyclopedias (it might be great if you have a set in your home: you're the judge).

The bottom line is, whenever your Little One asks a question; that time becomes a ***teachable moment***. If you are on-course, there will be no need for you to reinforce the fact that you are in charge; however, if needed, teachable moments are the times to sport the fact that "You da man." Either way, teachable moments are precious: you'll have tons of them, try to recognize and take advantage whenever possible.

That idea highlights the fact that your responsibility as the parent is not to be your child's friend. You are the guide, protector, and molder of your little "Bundle of Joy:" that comes first. On the other hand, if you perform it properly, you will be the partner of a powerful individual and a life-long friend.

Now, here's where I place a wrinkle in your tinkle: whenever you say "No" to anyone, including your Little One (even though you are his hero), it causes the mind to begin to snap shut and could produce the beginning of rebellion. Your primary concern should be to avoid being placed in a position that interferes with the content of your (and especially his) "barrel of fun;" in other words (please don't hate me for this), in spite of what I said about "issuing lots of no's" (don't tighten up on me now), **almost never, ever say "No."**

There, I've said it!

"Issuing lots of "No's," and "almost never, ever say "No," sure seems like a contradiction doesn't it? Not so! There are two sides to the "No" saga. The side that says "no" is the black/white side; that could be used directly to support conditions involving safety, health, behavior, and a host of other issues. That's the tiny side. The other side is where you need to practice and become proficient with Parent's Alternate Phrases to "no," I call them the PAP's.

When you become proficient with using PAP's, not only will you become unstoppable in molding your Little One into that little stick of dynamite, you will also maintain that "barrel of fun" of which we speak. For example, your Little One might ask, "Daddy, can I cross the street without holding your hand?" You might say, "<u>No</u>!" (safety issue). On the other hand, you could develop a PAP like, "Can a cow see her ass?" (Oops, sorry about that, that was one of my dad's favorite expressions: I couldn't resist).

Anyhow, I think you get the idea.

On second thought, in case you don't get the idea, let me stretch it out for you. During the times you are having loads of fun, practice PAPs with your Little One via "no-games;" in other words, on occasion during a lull in play time, or any time for that matter, start a game of saying "no." The way it works: identify a known feature that you know your Little One knows the obvious answer; for example, "Is the fleece on Mary's little lamb green?" The answer: Mary had a little lamb, its fleece was white as snow! Or, "Jack and Jill went up the hill to fetch a pail of water!" The "no-game" might be, "Did Jack and Jill go up the hill to fetch a pail of ice cream?"

Ah ha, now you get the idea! Have fun with it as you develop your favorite PAPs.

When it comes to developing PAP's, an entrepreneur named Chris Thompson has developed a technique (available on his website) that is absolutely incredible: it's easy and it works wonders. In fact, not only will it work wonders with your Little One, the technique will work with everybody you know, including your significant other. The link to his site is… Well, let's finish the third of the **three big things** first, then you can tap the link to his site. Just make a note, that way you won't interfere with the continuity of our effort here. However, don't forget: I guarantee you'll be amazed at the effectiveness of the PAP (Chris') technique!

Third, <u>**limit giving foreign objects**</u>: by foreign objects, I mean objects other than those that nature provides. If you refrain from giving your child too many toys, she will be more inclined to develop the inestimably important gift of imagination. I know that, if you can afford it, you probably will be tempted to provide generous numbers of toys. Give it some thought and consider this: experience has proven that children quickly lose interest in most toys. They are more intrigued with things that help them develop and exercise their imagination. Also keep in mind, the toys that your Little One leans toward the most will help you determine the nature of his life-long goals and desires (even when he might not be aware of them himself).

That's it for the "Three Big Things". See, that didn't take long, did it?

If you do them correctly, your Little One will begin to exhibit <u>self-discipline</u> at a much more consistent rate than otherwise. They are important because it causes your parent/child relationship to be much easier and much more fun. However, though the "big three things" are very important (it provides a non-threatening method of having fun with your Little One, at the same time instilling discipline), understanding and transferring the foundation of the **elements of the Factor of Five** is <u>essential</u>. Before we attack the core of this book we are going to tackle the **elements**, identify them as a package in a general context, wrap that package in a blanket of **discipline**, and use it as a foundation for the treatment of your "**Bridge to Success**."

Even before we do that, I didn't forget, let me give you the address of Chris Thompson's website (the PAPs), then you can come back here (we have just begun).

If it doesn't work, just cut and paste it to your browser.

http://www.talkingtotoddlers.com

Make a note: come back to page 15!

CHAPTER THREE

The Critical Three

Welcome back!

Before we get into the heart of identifying, and securing the **elements of the Factor of Five,** we need to magnify a support structure and place it into a secure foundation within the "Bridge to Success." Let me just say this: a full/successful relationship with your child requires a primary integration resident in supporting the pain of disappointment. In other words, the primary relationship with your child demands a belief in, and a relationship with, our Creator. Why? Because our souls hunger for meaning: "Why am I here?" "What is life all about?" "Why should I care?" The Bible and other similar books provide guidance and direction that satisfy that hunger. As a parent, it is essential that you provide your Little One with this saving foundation.

An atheist might say, "nonsense, prove it and I <u>might</u> believe it." Be that as it may, the fact is, emotion (cousin of spirituality) moves individuals with much greater efficiency and effectiveness than reason. In addition, I have never heard stories of individuals surviving extraordinary challenges, unscathed, except under the umbrella of spiritual belief.

The reason to establish a spiritual foundation is that life is full of change, and change often causes disappointment. None of us will avoid disappointment. Usually it surfaces because things we think we know, and/or understand, to our sudden confusion, amazement, or frustration, have changed. Our friends will disappoint us, our clergy will disappoint us, even our parents will disappoint us. Disappointments happen not because our associations intend them necessarily, and not because our expectations are unrealistic. The reason is, the nature of life demands that individuals change in response to changing conditions. However, many of us will be devastated when the awful head of that demon (change) occurs.

To be more specific: life is full of disappointments, they happen to all of us. The key is not what happens, it's what we do about what happens. Whether we are weak or strong, the most effective way to handle change is to seek and hold on to something that does not change. The problem with that is, the only thing which does not change is change itself. I know that sounds like the opposite of what we just stated: it is not, it is reality.

There is one exception: everything in this world changes; that is, everything material: everything that can be understood by our senses. However, things that cannot be comprehended by our senses do not change; our awareness of them may change, nevertheless, they are unchangeable.

The name for the unchangeable world is called spiritual or supernatural. A person can reach for and grab spiritual powers, and hold on for dear life. Here is one of the keys to internal happiness and serenity: *faith* is the power that binds our spiritual self to the real world. But *faith* is not easy to come by because it overrides belief and knowledge. Many convincing believers have dropped by the wayside under the assault of disappointment and change. In other words, *faith* in something or someone which does not change is the adhesive that binds one's strength and self-esteem to a foundation that will not waver or disappoint. Notice I said "faith in something or someone," in other words, the object of a person's faith must be identifiable and it must be personal.

Please allow me to add just one example of *faith*: when a person observes his time piece of reference (a clock, wristwatch, or whatever), his subsequent actions are based upon his belief that his timepiece is correct. In other words, whether the time is correct or not is not important; the fact is, his actions are the result of his *faith* that the timepiece is correct! Now exchange the timepiece with religious faith (Christianity, Islam, Hinduism, Buddhism, you name it): true or not, a person's actions reveal his *faith*.

On second thought, I want to add one more thing: within this work, I talk about morality and the goodness of the soul. I also am a believer of a higher power upon whom we can depend to bail us out when we have a problem seeing the forest because of the trees. Can we prove or disprove there is a deity? Only by inference and/or faith. An unnamed so-called comedian/talk-show host stated, (I'm paraphrasing) "To have faith is to refuse to think:" his audience applauded.

I'd just like to respond to that statement. We refuse to think about a ton of things every day of our lives; nevertheless, we can't see, hear, taste, smell, or feel many of them with our five senses. Does that mean they don't exist? When it comes to parenting, and molding a child to be the success he was created to be, you'll be pleased to know, "Bridge to Success" covers the essential formula: I call it the Factor or Five. I could rebut the so-called comedian, but I'll let you do it. On the other hand, he doesn't really matter: the success you and your child will achieve will counter anything and everything he believes or refuses to believe.

When I refer to the "Bridge to Success:" I mean you molding your child to be the success he was created to be. The key for you and he is to be totally honest with him and your life, and personalize the technique I reveal in this book. Everything else will fall into place: if you do it right, you and your Little One will have a "barrel of fun," and a ton of success.

I have placed the foundation of this book right here at the beginning because the real key to success in parenting or any other area of life starts in the heart and mind of the individual. So, without further ado, let's advance to our review of the **Factor of Five.**

The first component of the **Factor of Five** is LOVE. It is without question life's greatest experience. It is the emotion which serves as a safety valve. It helps relieve tension associated with self-discipline; in addition, it helps insure balance, poise and constructive effort. It also brings a person into communion with infinite intelligence and is the umbrella that shields and supports everything we do.

Writers of books, songs, poems and the like have attempted to define love or tell what it's all about. At this time, you want to identify, in **your** mind, exactly what Love is in the powerful context of parenting. From the standpoint of any relationship, Love is simply an image of the highest joy, where happiness reigns supreme. In other words, when a person says he loves someone or something, what really is happening is that the other person or thing causes him to feel that he is worthy of the positive way in which he projects himself in a garden of happiness. In still other words, that other person or thing reflects the inner image of his well-being and happiness.

To place that definition in context, a person might ask the question, "What does she mean when a she says, 'I love him?'" Could it mean that when she communicates with him it causes him to <u>feel</u> like she sees him the way he wants others to see him – the way he believes he really is? Keep in mind, at this point your Little One has no identity, that's what you are going to mold!

Here is another question: "He loves his pet." Could it mean that because his pet is excited to see him whenever he approaches her, she causes him to <u>feel</u> important and wanted? That might be one of the values of obtaining a pet, the pet will be non-judgmental.

How about: "He love his car/money." Could it be he treasures those things because when he has them, it causes other people to think he is a meaningful person and it makes him <u>feel</u> important and as worthy as he believes is? That's the value of establishing a cost versus worth lifestyle.

Not to beat a dead horse, but how about: "He loves to play basketball/racquetball/golf (any game/pastime)." Could it be that these things make him <u>feel</u> better physically? And when he competes, and wins, he feels important; especially when he is part of a team (mainly because man is a gregarious animal: we crave sharing ourselves with others who are like us).

Each of the scenarios above has one thing in common: <u>feelings</u>. But more than that, they signify feelings of importance, feelings that one's life is meaningful. That emotion is powerful because people are influenced, not so much by <u>what</u> happens to them as to how they <u>feel</u> about what happens. In the fabulously successful book "Think And Grow Rich" by Napoleon Hill, he gives us numerous reasons to embrace the idea that **creativity** of the mind is <u>set into action</u> entirely by how we <u>feel</u> (emotion), not by how we reason (think).

An interesting and related question about it (love) is, "How is it that a person can think in terms of falling in and out of love: are people merely fickle? Or is it simply that individuals are confused about the intimate nature of love?" I think it is the latter, so let's define it so it can fit any situation equally well: <u>mortal</u> LOVE is simply an image of personal worth.

When a woman says she loves a person, she means that person consistently elicits in her a feeling that she is worthy of the positive way in which she sees herself. To say it another way: to love a person or thing is to appreciate, admire and hold dearest, that which the person or thing repeatedly does to one's positive emotions.

Keep in mind, emotions are the mortal responses to material things that effect a person's bodily functions as well as attitude and perception, which effects behavior.

Love is not a desire, it is not a lusting or coupling of two bodies, it is simply the word we use to denote the highest in appreciation that causes us to feel the ultimate in personal gratification. The problem is, people have needs, and their needs constantly change. As needs change, so do the things they hold dear. Yet the things they hold dear at one stage in life have a tendency to change as well. Hence, the person says she has fallen in/out of love.

It's important to note, we're not talking about eternal love, that'll not change; that's the one linked with the Almighty Creator, which means, anything we do has no effect on it. However, we can utilize the effects of mortal love by understanding its link to you and your child (and the rest of us mortals). To do that, we need to understand and relate that mortal love has no significant personal meaning unless we share it with someone else.

At this point we want to back up and relate the first of our big three things ("talk/listen a lot"). At first, nearly all the words you use will have practically no meaning to your Little One; it's what you do and how you do it that is most significant. As time advances, words become more and more significant. With that in mind, I want to highlight the fact that our goal is to expand and invigorate **your** mindset to the degree that your words are consistent with your action. When that happens, the intense observation skills of your Little One will pick up on the real you; which means, the molding process will be most effectively embraced.

We talked about caring, mainly because it is one of the important components of love with consistency. To impose your mindset on your

Little One requires style, finesse, and adherence to nature's signals. An example might be that our creator has provided us with one mouth, two eyes, and two ears; which might indicate that we should speak about what we see and hear, about half as much as what we actually see and/or hear. With that in mind, it might bode us well that when we feel the need to tell our Little One to stop talking, to say: "I love to hear you talk, sweetheart (positive reinforcement), but there is a time and place that is appropriate. Now is not it." (or however you would express that idea, in a positive manner).

Remember we said, "Love is simply an image of the highest joy, where happiness reigns supreme." We traveled further into the definition, but didn't talk about some of the components of love that lead to success, let's do that now.

We talked about caring, but we didn't talk about "PASSION." My dictionary of reference defines "passion" as "boundless enthusiasm." The combination of discipline, love, and passion results in success on a grand scale. If we nail in one final ingredient we will open the door to a formula for success that cannot fail. That ingredient is PERSISTENCE.

Former President Calvin Coolidge ("Taciturn Cal") has been credited with nailing down an important proposition when he said, *"Nothing in the world can take the place of Persistence. Talent will not; nothing is more common than unsuccessful men with talent. Genius will not; unrewarded genius is almost a proverb. Education will not; the world is full of educated derelicts. Persistence and determination alone are omnipotent. The slogan 'Press On' has solved and always will solve the problems of the human race."*

In other words: practice, practice, practice (with an eye toward perfection). Keep in mind, practice can be boring; on the other hand, don't fall into the trap of cutting it too short. Use our key indicator: **progress** plus **smile index** (SI) equals possible elimination or continuation of the activity; on the other hand, whichever the case, don't make the sessions too lengthy or too short. How do you know? Your observation holds the key: the smile index might be a clue.

Now! Let's peak back into this element of success so we can really get a good look at it. If persistence is so important, how can we make sure our Little One will persist? The answer is, we can't, but we can be observant and hone in on what gives him the greatest joy, where (to him) happiness reigns supreme.

For example, one parent highlighted her success and how she revels in the joy of her children's discovery. She said, "Each of my children have chosen career paths based on interests they showed early on. My oldest child is an artist and has been drawing and creating since she was a baby. I found old essays my youngest wrote when she was little in school where she stated she wanted to be a singer and dancer/actress. She is in LA doing just that and my son has always wanted to be writer. He is studying writing in college and has tremendous talent."

That's a significant comment from a proud and successful parent!

"What if my Little One is pursuing the wrong thing?" Good question, here is one answer: teach him to establish goals and benchmarks; that way adjustments can be made along the way toward achieving his goal: plus, the tendency to discontinue the pursuit too soon will not raise its ugly head. The important thing is to understand it's not so much what you say, as to what you do. For example, let's say it takes thirty minutes to stroll to your local lake to fish; and let's say, the lake is ten streets from home. That means it'll take an average of three minutes to traverse the distance from one street to the next. The benchmarks would be three minutes each, or thirty minutes.

With that knowledge in hand, simply relate to your Little One, "When we want to go to the lake to fish, we know it'll take one hour just in travel-time to get there and back home because there are ten streets and it'll take three minutes per street." Then you can add, "If we want to make it forty minutes travel time, we can clock two minutes per street." (at first he'll ask, "What is a minute dad?"). Ha! Thought you had me didn't you? Yep, It'll take a little while before benchmarks become relevant to your Little One; select any other example of choice, but when it happens you'll be prepared!

You'll often hear me say, "Keep in mind…", it's just my means of reminding you that at first your Little One knows nothing about anything, he is simply a "Bundle of Joy," to him everything is new and challenging. His primary objective is to please you; however, also keep in mind, you can't continually fake him out, because he will always gravitate toward things that are natural to him, things that provide pleasure because they tend to aid in completing his wholeness.

When talking about "faking him out," this might be the ideal time to address the idea of Santa Claus. At some point, your Little One will be told, "There is no Santa Claus, your parents have been lying to you all this time!" One must admit, that's a serious accusation. The question is, how do we handle it? My response is, you be the judge!

However, my suggestion is to treat it the same as any other question-behind-the-question challenge. In other words, tell the truth in a natural way. Just as money and the Star Spangled Banner are positive symbols of independence, Santa Clause is a positive symbol of "love, goodness and kindness": however, only a symbol. Just as the heart of the Christmas religion is based on love and kindness, so is the idea of Santa Claus. That's the reason it is linked with the birth of Jesus Christ, (he is the soul of love, goodness and kindness).

The bottom line is, by the age of three years (again, you be the judge: it could be more or less time) plan to admit to your Little One that Santa Clause is real, relate to him that his other name is "With Love from your fellow man." Add to that the unearthing of realism that you will continue to celebrate Christmas via Santa Claus and have fun doing it. Also make it a point to reveal to him to not spoil the Christmas story (related to Santa Claus) for other children.

The value of this is that honesty will prevail with your Little One and any questions about the Christmas scene can easily be addressed and put to bed.

To continue: you, the parent, can determine the nature of your child's inclination toward his greatest joy. That's accomplished by providing a wide variety of mental and physical actions: they come under the heading of games. The playground provides the outlook to determine what he is inclined to pursue physically: that's where he swings, runs, jumps, kicks, throws, catches, etc. (body enrichment). The "kitchen table" is the venue for the mental, that's where he colors pictures with crayons/markers, plays cards, checkers/chess, board games, establishes computer skills, etc. (mind enrichment).

But, what does that have to do with love? you might ask. The answer is, not all children want to be athletes, astronauts, policemen, firemen, etc.; on the other hand, neither do all children desire to be chess champions, scientists, computer programmers. etc. Your goal as the parent is to make the job of parenting as easy and as effective as possible. That's accomplished by coalescing (or fusing) stages of the molding process into a way of life. The end goal is to provide balance in the life of your child.

Stage one is to determine the primary mental and physical inclination of your child. If he is inclined to be more mental than physical, then reduce the playground time and increase the "kitchen table" time, and vice versa. Don't eliminate either one, because your goal (say it again) is to provide a balanced child: one who will feel at home regardless of environment or circumstances.

Stage two is to further synthesize your child's inclination; for example, if he is more physical, does he move toward being more adept with use of the upper part of his body than the lower? Ask the question: is he inclined to throw and catch as opposed to kick and tumble, or vice versa? It's easy, all you need to do is be observant!

Stage three is to take advantage of his natural inclinations to enjoy being alive by finding or inventing games that you and he can share. The games should be established, when possible, under the banner of primary, secondary, and tertiary inclinations. The number one goal is to have fun, regardless of the game: if it's not fun for your child, discard it and move to something else.

Remember, our Creator has provided each of us with everything we need to gain anything and everything we desire (no exception). Now, it's your turn, your responsibility to make it happen! The single most important thing is, "Make it happen and make it fun."

At this point I'm at somewhat of a crossroads; in other words, I want to invest our time judiciously. That being said, I dislike going on and on because our precious time is the one thing that cannot be replaced. What I usually say is "The magic of this 'Bridge to Success' is that when you personalize your input, you make it yours: you individualize it and obtain more suitable and more lasting results." But, that might be viewed as a copout.

On one hand, tons of individuals have asked me to increase ideas on how to insure the bonding process continues at a good rate. On the other hand, many of you have had enough: if that's the case, simply skip to the next area of the **critical three**: "sex" (page 28).

I guess you'd say, I'm somewhat on the teeter-totter about going on; on the other hand, with some of you, some things are so important that if I miss them, I will have failed to close the gap and nail the container shut. With that in mind, without further ado, let's hit it!

When we open our container of love, hopefully you will exclaim, "That's it: that closes the gap for me!" So, here we go: remember we said your Little One wants to be just like you (that's true even if you are evil, heaven forbid), it's in your best interest and his, to share your success-secrets with him when you are "doing your thing."

In other words, from the business point of view; if you are a hole-digger, you already know how to dig the best and most beautiful hole (if you don't, shame on you); show him the easiest and best way to dig a masterful hole. If you are a secretary, teach him how to type or establish the most effective way to take notes. If you are an auto mechanic, teach him how to repair an automobile: maybe start with keeping it clean by washing it inside and out, and waxing it so that it looks absolutely sensational.

If he shows great interest, you may want to continue by showing him how to change a tire, plus identify the positive effects of acquiring good tires. Then, since the tires are off, talk about the brakes, and how and why they are important. Don't go overboard with this, and don't do it too soon (you'll know when and if, it's appropriate): I think you get the idea. The point here is, your Little One's hero (you) can naturally reinforce the role as "Leader of the Pack," and further solidify the bonding and molding aspect.

On the other hand, if your craft is more from a leadership standpoint, teach him how to be a convincing speaker, the principles of leadership, the art of negotiation, etc. Also, if you are in a position to allow him to sit in on some of your meetings, don't shy away from doing so (by all means, if and when appropriate). The idea is, any and all such activity will reinforce your march along the "Bridge to Success."

Looking at the situation from the home-front: If you see a problem around the house or apartment (as we all well know, there is always something), identify it, reveal the problem to him, and explain why it's a problem. Then let him accompany you and, indeed "aid" you, when you attempt to fix it. Be careful with this one though: some things may not qualify as problem-solving to be shared with your Little One. Safety might be one, the fact that your Little One is simply not mature enough, might be another; however, there is always something that you can incorporate in your daily, weekly or monthly routine that will help you further bond with your Little One and enhance the molding process.

Preparing a meal or snack is always an excellent selection (keep in mind, you want to do it with the <u>primary</u> goal of enjoying the before, during, and after the event). Even in the waning years of my dad's life (at that time, he was a widower), we would share a meal and look forward to obtaining the ingredients; sharing in the preparation, and enjoying the resulting goodness was a major part of our sharing. The goodness was more than the meal, it was more the sharing with my hero (yep, he was still my hero). The matter could be something as simple as making a milk shake, cooking a steak or hamburger, cornbread, cake: you name it. The important thing is the continued bonding.

If you are a ballplayer, chances are you will never be the best there ever was, but who knows, maybe he <u>can</u> be if you reveal to him the secret of enjoying being the best you, you can be. On the other hand, maybe you don't desire to be a great ballplayer, but there is no doubt you do it to have fun: show him how and why you obtain the greatest enjoyment from your activity.

If knitting/crocheting/sewing turns you on: if the bridge club, poker, cards of any sort: checkers/chess/scrabble attract you (get the idea?), whatever turns you on, share it with your Little One, and do it together. On the other hand, maybe he doesn't bubble up to anything that floats your boat: no problem, remember what we said about the smile index (SI)? That's your connective link, use it as your attachment to the "love boat."

No need to beat a dead horse, I think you get the idea: the time spent with your child will not always be fun and games; however, when both of you can look forward to any time together as a special capsule of life as a barrel of fun, and look back on memories that identify special times because it's with a very special person, you will know in your heart and mind that "Love is Timeless."

Darnit! One final final! If our benchmarks indicate we are on the wrong path, persistence might be harmful; keep in mind, that's why setting goals, careful planning and benchmarks are essential. *With that in mind,* Let's assume we are on the correct path.

To continue: use other words, with "Taciturn Cal's" idea: practice, practice, practice (with an eye toward perfection). Let's back into this element of success so we can really get a good look at it.

If persistence is so important, how can we make sure our Little One will persist? If you are with me, we agreed, the answer is, we can't! Having said that, here is a point you might want to consider: to expect your Little One to persist, you know that attribute requires discipline. Right? Right! But what if he's chasing the wrong weasel? Good question. The answer is, teach him to set goals, and provide benchmarks to measure his effectiveness. This will be extremely brief because it infringes on the next area of the critical three; plus he is less than five years of age!

For example, let's say he wants to have one dollar saved by the end of the month; the benchmarks could be, end of one week, (in his own words) "I will have saved $0.25." Second benchmark: end of week two, "I will have saved $0.50." Third benchmark: end of third week, "I will have saved $0.75." End of the month, "I will have saved one dollar." Then leave it alone – except at each benchmark, ask, "How are we doing son, where do you stand toward achieving your goal?"

If he's doing significantly better, never suggest he increase his goal; however, congratulate him and, in your own inimitable way, identify the fact that appropriate goals are those that are a little beyond what he thinks he can easily achieve. On the other hand, if he's lagging behind, never decrease his goal, simply suggest he adjust the degree of his benchmarks (which means, whether he realizes it or not, he will have to work a little harder to achieve his goal). Remember, be consistent, but take it easy, it's simply a means of molding a mindset.

Again, I don't want to beat a dead horse; however, keep the benchmarks span of duration extremely short – remember, this is simply a means of establishing a foundation: an idea in your Little One's mind. If it happens that he is lagging behind the benchmark you and he have established, show him how to make adjustments on the way to achieving his goal (it's important to highlight, if necessary, that he adjust the benchmark, but that he not change the goal at that point!).

Here is where it could get complicated: the above just might eat into having fun: if that's the case, scrap it. We must remember, your Little One knows nothing about anything, he is simply… (a vessel you can mold to provide success in all that he pursues). To him, everything is new and challenging. I've said it before, and you'll hear it again, his primary objective is to please you; however, you can't fake him out, he will always gravitate toward things that are natural to him, things that provide pleasure because they tend to complete his wholeness.

Remember, the Creator has provided each of us with everything we need to gain anything and everything we desire (no exception). Now, it's your turn, your responsibility as the parent, to "make it happen and make it fun."

I'll say it one more time (because I think it is that important) The time spent with your child will not always be fun and games; however, when both of you can look forward to any time together as a special capsule of life as a "barrel of fun," and look back on memories that identify special times because it's with a very special person, you will know in your heart and mind that "Love is Timeless."

The next time we talk about bridging the gap between infancy and adulthood (in the context of love), we'll not need to connect the dots between love, discipline, passion, and persistence, because we already have. It might be comforting to remember, parenting, like love, is a gift that keeps on giving.

Finally, isn't it exciting to remember the thing that makes it so easy to be a good parent is that from his emergence into our world, your little **"Bundle of Joy"** is **totally** dependent on you for his survival and pleasure. When you carry him out-and-about among the world (planning to go fishing, for example), be proud of the fact that you are responsible for being a caregiver and molder of a new arrival. Don't be afraid to show him off to friends and strangers alike: in fact, smile and revel in it; it will cause you and him to feel that he is something special and meaningful to you and the rest of the world – and he is.

Meanwhile, you will share and understand that he is adoringly <u>observing</u> your ability to do things that he can only hope one day he can do: simple things such as <u>sitting</u>, <u>standing</u>, and then <u>walking</u>, <u>running</u>, and <u>tumbling</u>. He doesn't know it yet, but you know one day he will be able to talk, walk, and be as physically adjusted as you; maybe even more so. In the meantime your adoring Little One will do anything you say (that's why it is easy to be a successful parent) because, at first, **you are his Superman and he wants to be just like you**.

Now, the second component of the critical three! Sex!

The second component of the **critical three** is SEX. It is also an emotion, the difference is that love comes in two varieties: spiritual and biological. Sex is biological only. It rests upon the axiom that the human mentality is designed to seek pleasure and avoid pain. This is where it often becomes difficult to separate feelings from logic, because sometimes what we think should be painful turns out pleasurable. Likewise, what we think should be pleasurable turns out painful. This element of the critical three can be a fooler because it often is cause for severe problems later in life. You should be very careful to treat this issue of sex very carefully because, it is the most volatile of the **critical three**.

This is where your molding might get muddled: we just finished identifying the essence of love, now we are going to reveal how sex relates to your Little One.

It is important that you, the parent, realize that your Little One is no different than every other normal human being; that is, he has sexual feelings. When you are in the sex mode you want to be sure you relate that a positive attitude toward sex means accepting sexual urges as vital and proper. It further means, those feelings should not be perceived as shameful; in fact, it means a healthy outlook is based upon his sexual identity.

Have you ever observed an infant crawling on cement or cinder blocks with no apparent feeling of pain? Have you heard of adults walking on burning cinders without getting burned, or feeling no pain from the intense heat? Conversely, have you heard of individuals gaining pleasure from being beaten? These are not uncommon events.

The fact is, the mind determines what is painful and pleasurable based upon the needs of the individual, and, little by little, needs are constantly changing. Keep in mind primarily, feelings of pleasure and pain are derived from the five senses: what we see, hear, smell, taste, and/or touch (feel). However, what titillates one person might irritate another. In fact, the same thing that titillates/irritates a person at one time might irritate/titillate the same person at different times.

Input from the five senses is the same for all of us: however, when it comes to the reproductive organs, there is a universality of pleasure; we call it sexuality and sensuality.

Every "normal" human being has sexual feelings; however, a good, clean, healthy outlook about your Little One's sex and his sexual role is formed from the minute of birth. In her extraordinary book titled, "Your Childs Self-Esteem," Dorothy Corkille Briggs talks about the wedding of sex and love, and how a child's attitude toward sex is formed from birth.

She doesn't use the term "hugs and kisses" exactly, but her meaning is the same. Obviously she and I are in agreement when we say each time you provide hugs and kisses, rock, pat, bathe, and feed your Little One, you provide an experience of taking in love. How he is touched and treated affects whether he finds physical contact pleasurable or not; it influences his future capacity to enjoy intimacy. The importance of this cannot be overstated. Hugs and kisses, and respect for your Little One's body and his needs, are his first exposure to love, and therefore to sex education.

If the attitude towards sex is distorted, the sexual pleasures derived from associations with others can be misinterpreted and often create immense mental and physical problems. Separately, sex and love are emotions with many sides, shades, and colors; however, the most intense and burning of all kinds of sex, is experienced in the blending with it of love. With that in mind, let's take it from the beginning and consider that the concept of pleasure and pain, relating to the reproductive organs, has a significant core that rests upon physical hygiene.

From the very beginning, clean your little one at least once daily. During the cleansing, <u>when appropriate</u>, teach her how to clean herself, and what each part of the body is reserved for, especially the reproductive organs. That part is extremely important; however, it is also extremely sensitive. In fact, it is so sensitive that the parent or primary care-giver should be the only one to engage in that phase of your child's education. Later, it will be easier to support a foundation of physical and mental health, plus sexual awareness, power, and responsibility.

Parents have been taught that the time to talk to their offspring about sex ("the birds and bees") is during puberty; not so, that's too late. Sex is a natural part of the human psyche, so we should approach it in a natural way. The importance of this phase of development cannot be over-stated: it is the most sensitive and far-reaching of any in the lifetime of your Little One. One more thing: the key to sexual development is to treat it as a natural occurrence, and do it from the beginning.

It is also important that we instill in her the idea that the size of a person is not necessarily indicative of strength, including the reproductive organs. Just like everything else, strength emanates from the mind. If the mind is clean, everything else will fall into place in a welcome sequence of events. The most important strength is not sexual strength, that'll come automatically if one pursues strength of character.

Now the big question: why should a book on parenting be concerned with the matter of sex? Good question! My answer is: the two major commodities of emotion are love and sex: the world is ruled, and the destiny of civilization is established, by human emotion. When we talk about Love, it is without question life's greatest experience. It brings a person into communion with infinite intelligence and is the umbrella that shields and supports everything we do; however, if not integrated with eternal and traditional love, sexual gratification is the emotion that can invade and interfere with the overall strength of your child.

I don't like the way that sounds: what I want to say is, you want your Little One to understand that both love and the special feelings that sexual gratification produces are special, yet the two are different, they should be placed in separate compartments of exposure. On the other hand, the two should be integrated. In other words, sex can distort the purity of love and cause your Little One to mistake the senses-altering matter of sex with it (love).

Doggonit, I still don't like the way that sounds. Obviously, the matter can be complicated; nevertheless, in my mind the bottom line is, you should be seeking to mold your Little One into an individual who possesses the balance of emotion with reason, controlled by **self-discipline**. That way, the problem of confusing sex with love will not raise its ugly head. Remember, honestly identifying and sharing his internal wants and needs with you, and a significant other, is a key factor in his overall development and march along the "Bridge to Success". That's one of the reasons, when we talked about the **three big things,** the first is to **talk and listen a lot**. The other side of that is to obtain a response from him! To close out this phase of the equation, the parent needs to act (TLA): it's easy to remember, just **talk, listen, and act**! on your instincts.

In addition, there is no doubt that the most powerful of all human emotions is sex. In his ground-breaking book, "Think and Grow Rich," Napoleon Hill said, and I agree, there is no doubt that there are other mind stimulants, but not one of them, nor all of them combined, can equal the driving power of sex. The major difference between the emotion of love and the emotion of sex is that love is spiritual **and** biological while sex is biological **only**. With your guidance, as your Little One progresses naturally, both the biological and spiritual can blend into a powerhouse of individual dexterity.

When the emotion of love is mixed with the emotion of sex, it will tend to guide a person's actions toward greater balance, sanity, and reason. There is no doubt that love and sex are both emotions capable of driving individuals to heights of super achievement, when we add a passionately idealistic attachment of two people (romance) to the mix, a person can become absolutely unstoppable.

When combined, those three emotions (love, sex, romance) may lift a person to the position of super-human. Then when the three are combined with the aid of discipline, it will lead your child far up the ladder of creative effort and success. The result is an achievement-building mastermind. Why? Because when the emotions of those three are combined with discipline, the obstruction between the finite mind of man and infinite intelligence are removed. When that happens, we can expect a powerful, unstoppable yet caring individual.

You are might be thinking, "He keeps saying the same thing over and over, does he think I'm a dummy?" Not at all, I just don't like the way I'm blending what I'm trying to relate: hopefully you get the idea.

Teach your Little One that her reproductive organs are "private," because that part of her anatomy is reserved for her and her alone: not her parents, not the embodiment of her religious faith, not her brothers, sisters, or neighbors, but for her alone. Teach her that her "privates" are designed to reproduce a human being just like her, and that her Creator was kind enough to provide pleasure during the act resulting in reproduction. The key to this and any other lesson is to keep it simple, keep it natural, and keep it with an element of fun. Parenting is a serious matter; however, don't be too serious, be ready to laugh, but only when appropriate.

Teach her that everything in existence is good; on the other hand, everything can cause bad results if used inordinately past their practical usefulness (abused). In other words, things are simply objects: they are neither good nor bad. They become good or bad as a result of their use: misuse nearly always ends with unenviable results.

We can provide many examples of misuse: we all know objects like guns, knives, rope can aid an individual to save or take lives. In addition, things other than objects can cause abuse, such as misdirected emotions, misdirected attachments, etc. Be careful when molding your Little One: sexual inhibitions are simply the most volatile of the **Critical Three.** The object of your concern is to mold a balanced individual who will become a formidable force within the world she will encounter.

I said it before, you will hear it again: of the "Critical Three," The matter of SEX is the most volatile. Sex is healing, not because it is pleasurable (there is no doubt about that), but because the Creator made it that way. In His infinite wisdom, He did it that way so we would seek to participate in the process, that way we would be more inclined to procreate: thereby maintaining and increasing our kind (the human race).

The optimum association is that we would do it under the umbrella of LOVE. It so happens we humans seek to place our own little spin on quite a number of things in our lives: sex is no exception. No problem, it's just that we have identified love as an emotion, sex is also an emotion; both of them, tend to interfere with purity of heart and mind. Sex is healing; nevertheless, regardless of age or gender, when we talk about sex we've got to be very careful to keep it in perspective with an event.

Before we continue, let me just say this: Dorothy Corkille Briggs has produced the most impressive book on relating to your child than any I can recommend, the title is, "Your Child's Self-esteem." In that book, in chapter twenty-five, she titles it "The wedding of Sex and Love." Her book is so good that if you failed to follow this guide, she covers problems that otherwise might arise. As far as I can determine, there is nothing else comparable in print.

Before we get too wrapped up in this sex thing, let's keep in mind we are talking about your little "Bundle of Joy," from birth to five years of age. Oh yea! You almost forgot about that didn't you? You probably don't remember a comedian named Flip Wilson, he was a riot, had his own TV show back in the mid 1970's. His favorite line was "The devil made me do it." Well, I don't want to point fingers; however, the point is, don't allow you or your Little One to entertain that phrase: we know negative images might always hover around us; nevertheless, that reason ("The devil made me do it!") is an excuse: <u>unacceptable</u>.

Let me just reiterate: your Little One has no idea about the meaning of love, sex, money or any other thing we take for granted, he's just trying to establish his identity. He doesn't know if he is male, female, dog, cat, sock, shoe; he's just a sponge, soaking up the reality of life. He is looking to you to guide him on the paths of self-awareness. You have a choice: walk away from your parental obligation and allow someone else do it, or you can decide to be a parent.

I certainly wish to not be rude, but as a parent, you have a tremendous obligation to your Little One, yourself, and the rest of us to mold your child to be the best he was created to be. To aid you in completing that task is our mutual goal.

The number one thing your Little One should know is his/her gender: that's why we clothe our little boys in blue apparel and girls in pink. That color rampage is not for the infant, he doesn't know his head from his toe, his rear from his front, he simply wants to get started with his new life. The reality is, he is totally dependent on you (or someone like you) to "show him the ropes."

You might say, "So what's the big deal?" The big deal is you can step up to the plate and be the hero your Little One sees, or you can lower your head and allow someone else to replace you in his hall of fame. It means if you decide to take up the gauntlet and be that hero, you must seek to be as good a you as you can be. In other words, it's not just about your Little One, it's about your total family package, it's about building a tradition of excellence of whom your ancestors and progeny will be proud with whom to be identified.

"That makes a lot of sense," you say, but "What does sex have to do with it?" Good question! My answer is: determining one's sex is the first step in self-identity. It's quick and easy. The most important thing is that "Mother Nature" provides a tremendous supporting role, all we need do is cooperate with her lead. The fact that we are talking about sex, leads us to talk about the perversion of sex ("In a book on parenting?"). Yep! Let's cover that beast and put it to rest.

When it comes to sex, your Little One was created with a clean and uncluttered mind: he had no idea about perversion of it and its lethal effects. We know one of our goals is to enhance the value of self and how we relate to others: we also know that sexual perversion, AKA **pornography**, distorts the value of creation and its relationship to self-worth. With that in mind, I think it would be a pity to not cover it.

Remember when we were talking about your child and the birds and bees? We said talking about sex at puberty is too late. Remember that? We just glossed over it at that time because you were not ready for it. On second thought, maybe you were ready for it, it's just that I was so convincing (modest me) that you just accepted it and said, "That makes sense." Now, let's enter the inner sanctum of sexual awareness and worm out the details as to why it is true.

Your child (male and/or female) is going to discover that when he touches his genitals, he is going to become aware of a tingle of pleasure: you want to be sure that that natural sensation does not come as a surprise to him/her and that he understands why it is true. Allow me to reiterate that this is one of the most critical acts you, the parent, will ever encounter: the timing must come as a result of observation, intuition (gut reaction), and exposure of your child to the world around him; in addition, it must be a one on one encounter.

You will probably agree, the most effective one-on-one is dad with boy, mom with girl, but not necessarily, it's just that it'll be easier that way. The reason is the bonding aspect will be increased immeasurably because you can relate his/her genitals to yours. On the other hand, even if you are a single parent, and your Little One is the opposite gender, you can utilize many neutral examples of male/female interaction. The key is, when he shares personal feelings with you, he doesn't want, nor does he need judgment, logic, reasons, or advice. Regardless of how eloquent you are, he doesn't want/need his feelings brushed aside, denied, or taken lightly: what he wants/needs is, understanding from you, his superman.

Keep in mind regardless of age, sex, race, or environment, it's the search for understanding that makes anyone reveal feelings in the first place. When your Little One shares emotions with you, you must be very careful how you respond. If you respond in such a manner that he perceives that you understand his shared emotion, you have taken a giant step in the bonding process. Also, remember when we talked about our "Three Big Things," I said, talk a lot and, "three things should accompany the words: smile, look the infant in the eyes as you speak, and seek acknowledgement from him: it might be goos, ahs, or just a smile; nevertheless, that makes it a two way street."

When your TLA is successfully active and when your Little One perceives you understand and share his emotions, the two-way street will be full of traffic **both ways**! I think you will agree: that's exciting!

Generally, the optimum timing would be sometime after the first year, but before the third year (I know that's a wide span of time, but it's not cut in stone: it's up to you to be the judge).

To continue: you want your child to understand that our Creator loves us, His omnipotent genius reveals the truth that He made the act of re-creating the human body pleasurable, and that He did it for the distinct purpose of procreation, and to appreciate as well as revere the act of sexual intimacy. You want to be sure your Little One is aware that when he arrives at the juncture where he can mate with a being of the opposite gender, he will be able to cause nature to produce a person just like him. The idea is to foster an inner resolve that the desired result of sexual activity will be so special and overwhelming that the world will proclaim him a parent (just like you).

I know what you're thinking, and you're correct: it won't be easy, the timing will be suspect, the wording must be carefully phrased, and a host of other things. However, the sexual education of your Little One probably is the single most important phase of your parenting experience.

The bottom line is, you want your child to understand that sexual perversion is a dishonest attempt to gain pleasure at the expense of honest evaluation of self. In other words, when a person is honest, he knows he is special, he also knows that he is no more special than anyone else. What that means is, he will be able to perform some things better than a great number of other people: it also means a great number of people will be able to perform some things better than him. That includes all feelings: physical and emotional. The point is, when we attempt to fool "Mother Nature," we are unknowingly asking for pain. When we are dishonest, pain will surely follow, either from reduced pleasure (compared to the natural pleasure of nature), or increased pain.

Here is the key: a person's body is intricately designed by our Creator to provide us with utmost pleasure in and of itself: all parts of our bodies are connected in such a way that individually they can provide pleasure and/or pain. Simply stated, Honesty produces pleasure: dishonesty produces pain. In your own inimitable way, you want to share that major tidbit with your little "Bundle of Joy" (in a passionate manner). On the other hand, don't overdo it, but do be consistent and ongoing in your support of "Mother Nature." Your mindset is the key: when you, slowly but surely share that with your Little One, the result will be magical!

Enough said about sexual perversion. However, I do want to add one final thing about sex and your Little One: he has no idea about the ravages that pornographic events can provide, he simply knows that some things cause him pleasure and some cause pain. Just as is true with all of us, we seek pleasure and attempt to avoid pain (mental and physical). That's one reason corporal persuasion (when used judiciously) might be effective; on the other hand, when used in excess or as a means of punishment, it can be detrimental to the relationship with him.

You may disagree, but I guarantee you, there is never a need to punish your child (strong, but true statement). However, when the need arises, your responsibility in molding him to expect to be accountable for his actions is to activate painful consequences for appropriately dishonest actions.

Just as an aside (to close out the idea of identity): there was a piece in my local newspaper a few years ago that seems to nail it in place. It was about a racial matter that really shouldn't have been a matter at all, at any rate I'll quote it here. The writer said, "I'm an American. My skin is darker than many other Americans; in fact, some people call me black (my preference), some call me African-American, others call me Negro or colored, still others have other names for me (some nice and some not so nice). However, the names people use to identify me in their minds have nothing at all to do with who I am." He went on to talk about the issue at hand at that time.

True, that statement had nothing at all to do with your Little One except that it illustrates the idea that others can identify him in their minds, but that's not the key to his identity: what's important is how he identifies himself. Male or female is not the question, it's just that identifying one's gender is simply the first step on the path to self-identification. Remember, we are still talking about a being birth to five years of age. I repeat: regardless of age or gender, Sex is healing; nevertheless, when we talk about that subject, we've got to be very careful how we handle it.

That, my friend, wraps up the second of the **critical three** and leads us to the third decisive element in the parent's mindset: **finances**.

Before we discuss that final element, I think you deserve a little levity as a means of relaxation. With that in mind, I'll relate a brief joke. This one also relates to the value of understanding, or misunderstanding the words we use.

Caution: It's a little off-color, I hope no one is offended by it. Here it is:

"The boss was in a quandary. After a planning meeting, it was determined he had to fire somebody. It didn't take long to narrow it down to one of two people, Debra or Jack. It seemed like an impossible decision - they were both 'super' workers. Rather than flip a coin, he decided he would allow one of them to make fate the final arbiter; in other words, he decided to fire the first one who used the water-cooler the next morning.

After partying all night, Debra came in with a terrible hangover. She went to the water-cooler to take an aspirin. The boss approached her and said 'Debra, I've never done this before, but I have to lay you or Jack off'. Debra replied, 'I don't feel very well this morning boss, could you just jack-off?'"

The third component of the **critical three**, one of our major sources of difficulty, is **money**.

In all communications with your Little One, you should link the idea, and it should be from the beginning, that money is not the root of evil, nor is the love of money. I know what the Bible and other sources of guidance say about evil caused by the love of money, but that phrase came from a time when wealth was produced by the labor of slaves, and by conquest.

Before the existence of America, men praised their leaders as aristocrats of the sword, and aristocrats of birth: they despised the actual producers because they were "lowly" slaves, or traders and shopkeepers. America was the first nation to reverse that thinking, that's why our nation became the world's leader in practically everything.

The fact is (I said it before, and you'll hear it again), to love a thing is to know and cherish its nature; there is no exception. You should assure your little "Bundle of Joy" that loving or wanting money is not terribly important, because <u>money is made possible</u> only by those who produce goods and/or services. It is the material shape of the principle that men who deal with one another must do it by trade, and give value for value.

The most important aspect of money is its source, which is production. You should assure your little "Bundle of Joy" that money is simply a tool of exchange. It cannot exist unless there are goods produced and men able to produce them. When we accept money in payment for our effort, we do so only on the conviction that we will exchange it for the product of the effort of others. Money, the dollars and cents in our pockets and purses, is a token of honor, our claim upon the energy of the people who produce material ideas in the form of goods and services. You should continually attempt to engrain the above in the mind of your little "Bundle of Joy."

An important aspect of money is, to understand the nature of it and place it in its proper domain. Teach your Little One that for today's needs, eighty percent of our income is more than adequate to allow us to live happily and enjoy the fruits that life has to offer. The remaining twenty percent should be invested: we should share half of that twenty percent with an entity other than our family: that's right, give it away! Give it to a needy neighbor, a church, a charity, any worthy cause.

Another name for sharing the wealth is "tithing."

Tithing nails down the fact that money is not the end-all of exchange. It is the symbol of wealth, but only a symbol. In and of itself, it has no meaning and no value; it is simply the name and meaning of worthy production. The remaining ten percent should be invested in anticipation of our future growth. An example would be to save or pay for education, buy stocks or bonds, provide a loan toward a deserving venture that promises growth, etc.

Here is one of the most important parts that should be communicated to your little "Bundle of Joy:" An honest man is one who knows he cannot continually consume more than he has produced. In addition, teach him the value of non-material assets: integrity, character, compassion, honesty, honor, humor, kindness, respect, etc. More importantly, continually mold the idea and unmistakable fact that money will not purchase happiness for anybody who has no concept of what he wants. It will not give him a code of value if he has no idea of what to value, and it will not provide him with a purpose if he has evaded the choice of what to seek.

Keep in mind, the key to effectively molding your Little One is that your words are consistent with your action; in other words, verification of what you say is how you live your life: what you do is the key!

Money, albeit a powerful commodity, simply represents the power within us to produce valuable worldly goods that can be exchanged for the worldly goods of others. What that means to you, the parent, is that each of us is able, in some manner, to produce better-than-average results. Whatever that ability is, you should share it with your Little One, and incessantly emphasize the idea that she must continually seek to be the best she can be. That means she should consistently seek to produce the best that is within her and to become ever better. In addition, teach her to never, ever accept mediocrity.

Just as a brief aside: I painfully, remember the first and only time I ran a cross-country race; I was in the army. The race began and ended in a stadium. When we were near the end and came back into the stadium, I still had reserve, and I felt that I could have overcome the third runner in the race. All I had to do was push forward, but I said to myself that fourth was good enough.

That's a painful memory to this day; not because I failed to complete the race at number one (or in this instance #3), but because I failed to put forth the best that was within me. Every child should be taught that "good enough" is only good enough when he has put forth the best he has to offer, and even then he should seek to become ever better. You might ask why this is important... the answer is, this is the embryo of passion, and **passion** is one of the mainstays of joyful success.

We've stated a number of things about money: everything we've said about it is designed to open your mind to the concept of it and where it fits in crafting your Little One's "Bridge to Success". All this being said; remember, he has no idea about money, what it is and why it might be important. However, remember what we said about him being unusually observant. Regardless of your financial status, if you have money problems, not only does he see it, he can sense it. On the other hand, if money is your strong suit, and you are overly extravagant with it, that action de-values its significance.

On still another hand, if you hoard it and treat it as though you will never have enough; that sends a message to him that he'd better be extremely frugal and protective of it because it may be taken away at the drop of a hat. If you have already planted the seed that money is simply a tool of exchange; that the proper use of it is supported by the "cost versus worth theme", and further, that it is the product of production: that problem might already have been taken care of. That's simply another example of preventing a problem even before it raises its ugly head.

When it comes to money, your goal should be to reveal its nature: cost versus worth is the theme, production is the standard: tithing is the key that unlocks its value. Whatever you do, you want your Little One to be well balanced about it: to do that, he needs to have a joyful relationship with it's value.

You may think of money as something out in space, that it is separate from you; not so, money is the fruit of production and the essence of freedom. Your actions with it require an alignment with a personal value system. Mackay McNeill said it well, in her book titled, "The Intersection of Joy and Money:" my impression of what she stated, and I agree, is that as long as you treat your actions around money as separate from who you really are, your Little One will probably (at best) have a slow start coalescing money with joy. That too, kind of places a damper on that "barrel of fun" of which we place a great deal of importance.

We said money, albeit a powerful commodity, simply represents the power within us to produce valuable worldly goods that can be exchanged for the worldly goods of others. What that means to you, the parent, is that each of us is able, in some manner, to produce better than average results. Whatever your ability is, you should share it with your Little One, and incessantly emphasize the idea that she must continually seek to be the best she can be. That means she should consistently seek to produce the best that is within her and to attempt to become ever better. In addition, teach her to never, ever accept mediocrity. (No need to look back! Yep, I know, I said it before, but doggonit, it's supremely important and well worth repeating, so get off my case – oops, sorry, don't mean to offend you!)

Remember, she sees what you do in addition to what you say. That means, in your job (union or non-union: management or non-management), your home (with your spouse, girl/boy friend, child), your play (whatever sport or activity): you, you, you must never, ever accept mediocrity!

Just as an aside: I define "mediocrity" as "average." I contend that no one is average, each of us has unique strengths and weaknesses: which means, we are unique in who we are. That also means, whatever we want to do or be, we can make it so. However, there is a big BUT! There is a price for obtaining anything we desire, the BUT is: we must accept the reality that we must pay the price.

To continue: Here is one of the most important parts that should be communicated to your little "Bundle of Joy:" We also said this before: "an honest man is one who knows he cannot continually consume more than he has produced:" if a credit card is used, work toward paying it off no later than the next billing cycle (let your Little One see what you are doing).

In addition, teach him the value of character, compassion, honesty, honor, humor, kindness, respect, etc. More importantly, continually mold the idea and unmistakable fact that money will not purchase happiness for anybody who has no concept of what he wants. It will not give him a code of value if he has no idea of what to value, and it will not provide him with a purpose if he has evaded the choice of what to seek. (Yep, ya got me again, I said it before -- but again, it is really that important).

Now, here's an idea you might consider: talk with your Little One about something special that he or you want to do or buy, place a monetary value on it: make it something that's small, within reach by the end of the month (you can make it a shorter or longer period, but it's simply a process to establish a mindset, so about a month is probably the best time-frame). At the end of each week, you and he arrange to place one fourth of the agreed upon sum in a drawer, under the mattress, in a sock or shoe (anyplace becomes "a special place:" no big deal, but make it obvious). Then, at the end of the month, celebrate your achievement by doing, or buying what you planned to do or buy (maybe a special dinner out, or some special congratulatory ritual).

You don't need to do that a bunch of times to embed the concept within your Little One of living within your means, setting goals, planning to achieve them and celebrating the result.

The secret is to do all the above with style and finesse; in other words, don't be extremely obvious; on the other hand, let it all hang out. Like we said about yes/no when referring to tough love, it's better to say we can wait to get it later (when we can afford it) than to say "Put it on the card."

I was going to wait and place this next idea in Part Two, the action section, but then I decided it might be a stronger suit in the hands of your mindset. With that thought in mind, I decided to place it in both places. You may think this idea is premature, and you may be correct; however, if you decide to do it, I recommend you implement it no earlier than the first birthday and no later than the third (you be the judge).

That being said, here's the idea: On his birthday, the present to him could be the following: a) a receptacle (hereafter called a "Piggy Bank"), b) one coin (called a unit, hereafter called an allowance (no less than a penny, no more than a dollar – no paper allowed), c) agreement that the "allowance" will be paid the same day the parent is paid for his productive effort by his employer (or announcement of the results of his investments), d) agreement that the accumulation of coins will be called the Little One's personal assets, to be disposed of when and/or if he desires (for any purpose: be sure he is aware that the money is his to do with whatever and whenever he wishes, the only stipulation is that the parent(s) knows in advance of his intended "extravagance").

Here's an additional point to accept, reject, or consider: add three more things: 1) keep a register of all credits & debits regarding his allowance (your Little One should not be aware of the register), 2) on the last day of each month, you could exchange units to make the numbers more manageable: 100 pennies is the same value as twenty nickels, ten dimes, four quarters, two halves, one dollar, etc., 3) Pennies to nickels the first month, then Nickels to dimes, quarters, halves, dollars: at the end of each month (one day only), you and your Little One might want to consider some kind of numbers game. Who knows, it might even advance to an investment game: whichever the case, it could come under the heading of "fun and games."

But, don't do the exchange all at once; for example, if the allowance is a penny a day, the last day of the month, he could exchange the pennies for six nickels. On the other hand, you might make it a game, let him be the decision-maker, "You want to keep the thirty pennies?, or since five pennies and one nickel is the same value, maybe you want to make it one nickel and 25 pennies. That way you can count 26 times instead 30 and have the same value; in fact, if you wanted to, you could count 6 times (with six nickels) instead of 30 and have the same value. Whatever you want to do is OK with me, it's your money!"

Isn't life great? It can be pretty simple too! Again, the secret is to do all the above with style and finesse; in other words, don't be extremely obvious, on the other hand, let it all hang out.

If the above floats **your** boat: that's great! The key is to have fun with your Little One. If it turns **him** on, great! On the other hand, if it produces no joy in Mudville, trash it! (It's your decision!)

Before I express my final word about money and finances, I've got a suggestion: if you are not already wealthy and less than forty years of age, get yourself a hunk of **term life insurance** from a solid insurance company: if or when you turn forty (not before), add a **whole life insurance** policy. In addition, have your employer immediately begin to deduct one dollar per day from your income and arrange to auto-invest in a financial vehicle that will compound your investment.

In addition, when you get a raise, increase your auto deductions accordingly. If you get paid weekly, that'll be five to seven dollars per week: monthly, about thirty dollars. Regardless of your financial condition, you'll not miss the funds in your current life; on the other hand, if any unplanned negative events happen to you, the financial care and attention to your Little One will be provided: it'll be on auto-pilot.

Here is the final word about money: the five year period, from birth of your Little One's path along the "Bridge to Success," is a "show and tell;" in other words, it just might mean revamping your Self-discipline -- **your** self-discipline -- **your** self-discipline (hiccup!).

CHAPTER FOUR

The Silent Spoiler

The preliminary discussion about **the critical three**: LOVE, SEX, and MONEY was brief but pointed. Before we enter the next leg of our **association,** there is one element of the parent's critical involvement that must not be overlooked: it is the matter of identifying the devil of emotions. I call it the *silent spoiler.*

To fully arm your Little One with ammunition to take advantage of the strength provided by erecting a foundation of the **critical three**, the parent must identify and turn the tables on the *silent spoiler*; namely, **FEAR**. Even though we know, if we couldn't be afraid, we wouldn't survive for long; nevertheless, fear is an emotion that can turn the tables on all the positive qualities of possessing the core strength of the **critical three**. For that reason we must attack it with vengeance.

Remember way back at the beginning of our effort, I said, "**Your mind has already been conditioned; in other words, you already have a foundation from which you are able to influence your little "Bundle of Joy." The magic of your relationship with him is that he has a clean slate: his mind is like a CD that has already been formatted, it's just waiting to receive data."** What that means is, you are the psychological mirror he uses to build his identity: in other words, his whole life is affected by the conclusions he draws from your identity. That is why we began our journey the way we did, with the "Three Big Things". And that's why I talk about your mindset and the importance of the Critical Three: Love, Sex, and Money.

Every individual is born without a sense of who he is. With that in mind, let's identify "The Silent Spoiler" and put it to rest. What is this thing called FEAR and what makes it so dangerous? Remember when we said, "**creativity** of the mind is <u>set into action</u> entirely by how we <u>feel</u> (emotion), not by how we reason (think)?" Well, FEAR can be a disabling emotion because it can cause paralysis of the senses to the degree that it can immobilize an individual, or at the very least stall the desire to act – we call that delayed action **procrastination**. People procrastinate for one reason and one reason only: uncertainty. The foundation of uncertainty is FEAR. So let's identify this demon and include it in our parenting skills.

The thing to realize and share with your Little One is that fear is simply a servant of intuition: it is intended to be very brief. True fear is a survival signal that sounds only in the presence of **potential danger**. It is only a thing that announces or indicates that something <u>may</u> cause us harm; in other words, it summons powerful predictive resources that tell us what might come next. Hence it is the thing that might happen next that we fear; that is, the thing we <u>link</u> to fear, not what is happening at that moment. Fear says <u>something **might** happen</u>. If it happens, we stop fearing it and start responding to it: in other words, we manage it or surrender to it.

Fear can be an ally; however, in the vast majority of instances, it is a monster negative that moves in delicate ways to destroy all that it touches. On the other hand it does not destroy negatives; on the contrary, it feeds them. Immoral acts are monster negatives and worthy allies of fear. The satisfying thing to remember is that there is nothing to fear if we endeavor to put forth the best that is within us one hundred percent of the time.

There is one more thing the parent must understand and identify. When a person is **insecure and uncertain** whether he can live up to what is expected of him or not, he will respond in one of two ways. He will tell the truth and let the chips fall where they may, or he will camouflage it so as to avoid confrontation. When camouflage happens he will make excuses or use violence to cover his perceived inadequacy. Response to insecurity is always the same: he will tell the truth or make excuses. That's important for the parent to know.

Here is the key that will disable the frightening effects of fear - this is what you, the parent, must impart to your Little One: when a person does what is moral and couples that with producing the best that is within her, there is absolutely nothing to fear, **ever**! Now, here is where we place another wrinkle in your tinkle: keep in mind, we are not talking about things that people normally fear; for example, rats, spiders, snakes, failure, death, etc. Identifying specific objects, thereby developing an understanding of that which we are afraid, goes a long way toward erasing that kind of fear. Any fear is of concern, but in the instance of parenting, we are talking about the soul of your Little One; his love, desire, intuition and the like.

I call FEAR the "Silent Spoiler" because it is not a positive element of our existence; it interferes with the successful understanding and control of the critical three. In other words, it tends to mute the parent's success. Let's look at the "Silent Spoiler" and delve into the means of insulating those essentials from their primary enemy.

FEAR emanates from one thing and one thing only: **insecurity**. I know we have said it before; the reason is to nail it down without uncertainty. Insecurity is generally the result of lack of facts and refusal to deal with reality. Now, before we continue, I'd love to give an example of at least one individual who is totally secure; that could be extremely difficult. So let's simply identify a person by title: the founder of a successful corporation like Bill Gates of Microsoft, or Thomas Edison, inventor of the light bulb, Arden Hayes, the little five-year-old lad (a guest on Jimmy Kimmel's late-night TV show). The reason is we are talking about your little one-to-five-year "Bundle of feelings," that's why it's so critical to first mold him into a powerful tool of identity.

A secure individual is one who feels good about himself, and those with whom he associates, has personal value attached to his identity, plus he has identified who he is. The complimentary component is that he promotes awareness indicative of becoming a worthy and productive citizen; a person who adds value to himself and his community.

Let's take our essentials one topic at a time; while we're doing it, keep in mind your goal is to understand, highlight, and expose ammunition to guard against losing gains from your successful entry of your Little One's **critical three mindset**.

Love; what is the nature of fear when love is involved? The very first thing we must do is identify what love is: we did that when we said, "Love is Timeless."

Keep in mind, when we talk about fear we're not talking about **eternal love**, that'll not change; which means, anything we do has no effect on it. However, we can utilize the effects of **mortal love** by understanding its link to you and your child (and the rest of us mortals). To do that, we need to understand that nothing has meaning unless we share it with someone else. In other words, fear can destroy the magic of a beautiful sunset, a warm summer cloudless night, a magical surrealistic performance of a supremely talented ice skater, ball player, painter, etc. Those things have no meaning unless shared with someone else. Therefore, teach your Little One to **not** allow the fear of rejection to cause him to fail to open dialogue with a potential companion (playmate). In many instances, simply smiling and saying "Hi," is enough to open a world of enjoyment with another individual.

Sex: we said it is healing. The first and most important item under the umbrella of sex is honesty; in other words, the manner in which a person approaches sexual awareness is to be honest. The key is to accept the uniqueness of self, and expose life's joys with the intent of sharing those joys with others in a natural and sharing manner. Realization that Nature provides many, many patterns of enjoying our physical and mental uniqueness can be a monumental achievement. Seek to recognize the beauty of the sunrise and sunset, smell the roses; appreciate the heavenly blinking of stars on a warm summer eve. Reveal to your Little One the emptiness of anything (including sex) without feelings of achievement in winning the heart of a loved one. Nail down the fact that fear can destroy all that is worthy (don't forget: in this scenario, your child is less than five years of age).

Money: we said it is only a symbol: the essence of it is production. It is simply the ability to produce positive results in order to exchange our efforts for the productive results of others. What is important in molding your child and enjoying all that life has to offer is that you identify his passion: the areas about which he is most enthusiastic.

Some say we need a college education to achieve success. Not so; however, a degree from an accredited institute of higher learning, indicates a degree of discipline. You know the importance of that ingredient. Fear of academic failure can cause that future to evaporate into nothingness on a park bench. Remember what we said when talking about effort: as long as we are moral and put forth our best effort, there is absolutely nothing to fear, ever. The primary weapon of fear in each of the "Critical Three" is honesty. That is the primary positive point of the Three Big Things: talk and listen a lot (talk, listen, and act).

Just to recap, we said "life is full of disappointments, they happen to all of us. The key is not what happens: it's what we do about what happens. Whether we are weak or strong, the most effective way to handle change is to seek and hold on to something that does not change." We covered change and disappointment back in chapter three; just as a refresher, you might want to review it before we continue.

Now, where were we? We were talking about reasons that fear may invade the love mindset, and how you can prepare your Little One to avoid it.

Primarily, the problem appears when love may change as conditions change. That's the one we identified as FEAR. Fear comes in all sizes and shapes. The first one is fear that the other person will not return his love. The key here is to always be honest, communicate (don't just use words: actually communicate), and be yourself. A person will love **you,** not who you think you would like to be. The strange thing is, if she loves **you,** she will attempt to help you become that other person you think you would like to become (that's weird, isn't it?). Just be honest and everything will work itself out.

Another reason for invasion of the Silent Spoiler could be, a person might think his love will take unfair advantage of him if she knows he loves her: she may meet someone else that turns her on more than he does. Other fears could be personal appearance issues (I'm not so sexy: I'm bald, I've got a bear gut), health issues (I smoke too much, my cough annoys potential mates), personal belief issues (political: I'm a liberal/conservative), religious (I'm an atheist, Christian, Muslim, etc.), sporting (my favorite team is the Cubs, Bengals, Celtics Bruins, etc.)…

There you go again: I know those are not examples of your Little One's concerns. Those examples are to simply used to set your mindset in motion. It's just that they all stem from insecurity, and all of them can be eliminated (that's right, Silent Spoilers can remain silent and fail to spoil your child's pursuit of happiness), if you, the parent, provide him with a solid foundation of self-discipline. Now, stay off my case! Ha! Thought you had me didn't ya?

All you need to do is guide him to be honest, be himself, and continue to expose his real self. You may not like the way that sounds, mainly because we usually define the word "expose" as meaning something undesirable or injurious, but it also means, introduction to something beneficial or positive. That's the one I mean.

In this instance, thanks to you, his parent, your Little One will have a ton of goodness to expose (share) with a potential companion. That's where the matter of happiness resides.

Some of the potential problems are obvious, but those akin to the silent spoiler are hidden beneath the rubble of dishonesty. You, the parent, should think about that as you mold your child into being a tower of power

From your point of view, love concerns can be resolved by the simple means of communicating, coupled with observation. That's why, talking to your Little One is so important. As we said before, at first, it doesn't matter what you say, just talk a lot; on the other hand, you want your Little One to respond. It could be goos, ahs, giggles, it doesn't really matter, but you want him to respond. As he begins to understand words, what you say becomes increasingly more important because words mean things. So be careful. The key is not necessarily what you say, it's what happens as a result of what you say, mingled with what you do. What you say and what you do should be, must be, consistent. If not, you might lose a sizable chunk of discipline and understanding to your Little One's mindset.

Not to beat a dead horse, but there is no question that words have power; in fact, they can aid in shredding or building your Little One's self respect. On the other hand, words must match true feelings. Self-respect and high self esteem doesn't come from buttering him up, on the contrary, nothing could be worse. Unless the words you use are consistent with your actions he will detect the discrepancy. Then he might be inclined to lean toward distrust because of the mixed message.

I need not remind you, the key to developing self-discipline is to impose discipline during stage one: use the three big things: "talk a lot, lot's of no's (when appropriate, don't forget: seek to become proficient with the PAPs), plenty of hugs and kisses." The longer we dally, the tougher it will be for your Little One to establish self-discipline.

Remember, the key ingredient in the "Bridge to Success" is discipline blanketed with Love. The goal is to mold him into a missile of self-discipline: that's the tough part. Remember, for every "no" there's a reason (there is also a PAP). PAPs make it easy for your Little One to understand and have fun with the "Why not." When you add the easy parts of love, respect, and fun, you've got yourself a new world.

Congratulations (in advance)!

One more thing about fear (yeh, I know, I keep adding to the trough, but this is also important or I wouldn't invest the time): teach your Little One to never be afraid to make decisions. In addition, relate to him he should never make important decisions casually, and never make them without conferring with someone who cares about his welfare; however, never be afraid of being wrong. Share the fact that, the quicker we decide, the quicker we will begin reaping the benefits if we are correct. On the other hand, if the decision is a poor one, we can quickly identify and adjust the error, and eliminate and/or reduce our losses.

One final final (I promise), stride to make the cost-versus-worth mindset a way of life. By doing that, it will place FEAR in its coffin and nail it shut!

To close out this matter of the silent spoiler, it might bode us well to quote from noted figures in history. One of the most practical quotes of all time was made by former president Theodore Roosevelt (FDR), when during "The Great Depression," and when Japan attacked us at Pearl Harbor he said: "The only thing we have to fear is fear itself (In other words: it's a mental thing)." Another quote comes from the British orator and statesman, Edmund Burke, he said, "No passion so effectually robs the mind of all its power of acting and reasoning as fear (again, it's a mental thing)." Enough said.

Simple and uncomplicated, that's one of the goals of this effort. We can propose little things a caregiver can do (even if finances are limited) that will make a big difference in molding a new arrival. Something as simple as talking to your Little One makes a big difference. That's one reason many parents have proposed **RAM Time** (the next chapter) to aid in establishing a moral and caring foundation of family cohesiveness. I've said it before, and you'll hear it again and again and again: Family time and the importance of the family cannot be overstated.

The parent is the child's first and most important teacher. To aid you, the parent, this book was written with the primary idea and purpose of enriching the strength and vitality of your child. Learning that takes place **before** your Little One starts formal schooling, is the solid foundation that will maintain a solid hold on reality. That time-frame sets the stage and prepares her for everything she learns in school, and in **life**. If we do it right, the result will last a lifetime. Not only that, she, plus her friends, neighbors and countrymen will gain immense satisfaction, security and pleasure because of it.

A child who is happy and displays a feeling of security; that is, one who is coupled with discipline and guidance toward that which is right and proper in a civilized society, is a child who will **choose** to develop the moral character that will propel her to heights of accomplishment she was created to achieve. You might be asking, "Why does that sound like an echo?" The answer is, repetition is essential because of the importance of the sub-topic.

Let me not tarry before completing our **Essentials of Successful Parenting's** final element so you can fully partake of the essence of this effort.

Even before we enter part two, you'll view your little "Bundle of Joy" a little differently and with eyes that light up with the joy of parenthood.

CHAPTER FIVE

RAM Time

Having strong family ties is an element of identity, meaning, strength and security: untold numbers of families use the model effectively. With this in mind, we begin our final **element** of parenting control and effectiveness (the **Factor of Five**). Many parents use the following method to varying degrees. Most individuals don't have a name for it, many do -- I call it **RAM Time**:

RAM Time is one of the most effective methods used to develop a strong, secure, and successful family which chooses to do that which is right and proper for themselves, their community, and the rest of the nation.

Some of you will elect to begin sooner or later; however, **now** is the ideal time to introduce *"RAM Time"* – **R**ituals/**R**ules **A**nd **M**orality guidance. A sense of right and wrong (morality) has to begin at home. It is at this time that your family, headed by you, the parent(s), should plan family code-of-conduct meetings. These meetings can accomplish at least three things that prevent problems ahead of time: **rituals**, **rules of behavior**, and **consequences.** Consequences are important because if the rituals/rules are not followed, the individual will pay a price to the rest of the family – not to a corrupt gang, the police, or courts.

The following guide is by no means "cut in stone." It is simply an outline, a sketch, a framework of a means of energizing and planting the seed of a strong family unit: a unit that protects and supports all that is meaningful for you and your Little One.

RAM Time rituals is the beginning of a formal family routine; it is designed to merge your Little One into the routine of your total family and community. The most appropriate setting is at the "dinner table," and the rituals should be specific. It is not always possible to establish a definite time for your "RAM-time dinner hour." If you are fortunate enough to provide it daily, that's fabulous -- do it. However, many of you will only be able to squeeze it in once a week -- that's a minimum. If that's where you stand, no problem --just do it.

I know you're busy, but you'll be surprised at how effective it will be to plan an entire week's "dinner-hour-meals" in advance – nothing elaborate. Even if it is sandwiches every day, on the weekends solicit suggestions from the rest of the family (no special individual dishes). Arrange it so that everyone will partake of the same menu items during the "dinner hour." If nothing else (regardless of your financial exposure, or lack of it), one of the things that does is to reduce expenses and keep you, the "leader of the pack," in tune with the idea of cost verses worth.

Point of interest: have you ever heard of a homeless family? You only hear of <u>individuals</u> who are homeless. Families always tend to bond together and share their success and failure; unfortunately, most of us can't avoid failure to some degree. The most impressive thing about this book is, it is designed to increase the likelihood of your Little One and your entire family, enjoying success to a greater degree than ever before.

Let's continue. We were talking about the dinner menu. Every Sunday night (or whichever day ends your week), post the menu on the "frig" (do it anyplace that all can easily see), it's simply a reminder to all: it might sound somewhat regimented, nevertheless successful parents have proven it works wonders.

In some instances, you may want to designate specific days for specific kinds of meals. When I was a child, we lived in "<u>the projects</u>" (government subsidized housing). Nevertheless, my family enjoyed fish on Friday, sandwiches on Saturday, and chicken and potato salad on Sunday. During the rest of the week my mom offered practically anything and everything. (Did you say, "Who cares?" – I agree… sort of)

First, let's address **Rituals**. There are two parts to the Rituals routine.

<u>**Part A**</u> is designed to instill morality and ethics in your Little One's mindset. The way you do that is to ask just three questions followed by "why?" (you can call it mentoring or whatever, but do it at least once per week).

For example: 1) "**What** did you do today (this week)?" ("That sounds like it might be fun:

(why) what made you think of that?"

2) "**What** did you do that caused you to feel the most satisfaction?"

(**Why**) "Do you think you'd like to do more of that?"

3) "**What** did you do that you kind of regret (maybe it made you feel sad)?"

(**Why**)"If that situation were to arise again, have you thought of a way to lessen the impact or eliminate the pain?"

Very important point: Complete very brief notes (after the session, not during it), date the notes and keep them in a secure binder: again, the notes should be extremely brief (only the salient points). Never have them visible during RAM time.

Part B is designed to share yourself with others (maybe even a different culture) along with your little "Bundle of Joy." If you are wealthy or well-off, you might want to interrelate with a family who struggles to make ends meet. If your family struggles to make ends meet, you might want to interrelate with a family who is well off or wealthy (Part B should be completed at least once each month). I know this can be tough, but the results can produce tremendous returns. Keep in mind, you are the boss: anything I say here is simply "food for thought;" nevertheless, our BOSP have proven successful returns.

To continue! The following are five suggested **RAM Time Rituals at the "dinner table."**

Rituals (Part A):

1) TV and radio (except background music) are to be avoided.
2) Eating by any individual should be started only after all are at the dinner table, and (this may be controversial) eating should begin only after the head of the family has given thanks that there is a meal to be had. The thanking is usually religious in nature ("thank God"), but it does not have to be (the atheist can thank whatever or whomever he believes is responsible for his

existence). The important thing is to guide your Little One in the path of understanding that there is a "force" higher than he is, that has allowed him and his family to be fortunate enough to have life-sustaining products available for their consumption.

3) Interruptions such as phone calls (inbound/outbound), or visitors should be postponed until after "**RAM Time**" has ended.

4) Everyone should remain at the dinner table until all are finished and the head of the family agrees that "RAM Time" has ended, and

5) (this is the most important part of "**RAM Time**"), everyone must participate in communicating with each other (not just talking, but really communicating).

The question might be asked, what should the family talk about? Actually, when you talk to your infant, what you say is not terribly important. Whether you like it or not, you teach your family (including your Little One) about right and wrong all the time by what you do, and how what you say relates to what you do. The point is, it is important that you **be consistent**, that your words match your actions. Also, it is important that the family seek to develop the habit of communicating with each other. When successful, you'll be surprised at how well things will work out.

Having said that, let me add one critical point. Regardless of the topic, the stance should be from a positive point of view. Your household should identify failure, but only as a learning tool. For example, a person could be victimized simply because he was in the wrong place or time. An interesting and thought-provoking discussion could be started by suggesting how a situation could have happened and how the resulting problem could have been avoided. The point is, the only thing that really matters is success instead of failure, heroes instead of victims, courage instead of cowardice, desire to achieve instead of acquiescence toward that which tends toward victimization.

Rituals: just an added comment about Part B. It was taken from just a handful of good/successful parents: however, you might agree or disagree that it could be an idea that can be shared in many beneficial ways. It's a matter of sharing the practical application of a different culture or lifestyle. Start with your Little One somewhere around nine months of age. If your position in life, in terms of financial resources, is middle class to wealthy, the culture-sharing should be among the poor to poorest of the poor. If your financial position is poor, the culture-sharing should be among the middle class to wealthy.

The sharing can easily be accomplished by attending services at a church, synagogue, mosque, or any house of worship (that way you can be fairly well assured the family believes there is a force higher than themselves to which they are accountable).

At an opportune time, usually before or after the services, introduce yourself and your Little One to one or more members of the congregation who has a child of similar age. The goal is to develop an association with a different family who enjoys the same (or even a different) lifestyle than you and your Little One. The other family may have more than one child within their household that fits the standard of your objective; nevertheless, it is important that you include only your little "Bundle of Joy." If your position is that you have more than one preschooler, you might consider taking the other one(s) to a different house of worship and completing the same action.

After completing a session of Part B Rituals, the RAM Time dinner table might tend to be even more interesting, informative, and educational than usual.

One last thing about Rituals: they should apply to each family member and/or guest(s).

There should also be **rules of behavior** to apply at all times including "**RAM Time**." The following are **six suggested rules of behavior**, each of which is stated as a prohibition:

1) Lying/cheating is prohibited
   (Reason: the liar becomes a victim of the person to whom he lies);
2) Crude and/or profane language is prohibited
   Reason: use of such language in formal settings indicates lack of breeding and intelligence; on the other hand, keep in mind that this is a routine that is designed to secure family and community togetherness. Use of crude and/or profane language might be part of your culture and it might be included

as part of your survival mode. If that's true, acknowledge it, at the same time keep in mind that your goal is to build a strong fortress of successful family values. This could be a tough one: your culture (environment) might demand that you act a certain way for your immediate survival. Keep that in mind. Nevertheless, survival mode has nothing to do with your upward mobility.

3) Physical contact with the intent of hurting another person without cause is prohibited.
Reason: it indicates weakness and insecurity, plus it could increase the number of people who may want to harm you.

4) Taking another person's possessions without permission is prohibited.
Reason: that is stealing: winners don't steal, they earn.

5) Rewards must be earned.
Reason: production of assets builds character, integrity and material wealth.

6) Inappropriate behavior is prohibited (appropriate behavior should be established and/or defined, and agreed upon by the entire family).

Rules can easily be established during the beginning stages of **RAM Time,** or parents can establish the rules and hone them to fit their family needs and purpose.

Now comes the matter of **consequences**. The establishment of consequences is probably the most important part of the rituals/rules saga, and they should be established as an agreed upon result of unacceptable behavior. You might ask, "Agreed upon by whom?" The answer is, agreed upon (without coercion) by each family member **before** an incident happens (that means, they must be general and all-encompassing). Keep this important point in mind: your actions of following through, or failing to follow through, on these rituals/rules/consequences, sends a powerful and vital learning message to your Little One: a message that lasts a lifetime. However, one point of caution: don't be so black and white, so died-in-the-wool stodgy, that you can't be reasonable and empathetic. On the other hand, don't be so liberal that you accept any reason as satisfactory! Nearly every reason is merely an excuse (unjustified explanation of improper behavior: <u>unacceptable</u>).

Maybe you believe in God and maybe you don't. Whichever the case, I think you will appreciate the way Scott Cooper talks about right and wrong in his book titled, "God at the Kitchen Table." Of particular interest might be the section titled, "Informal conversations: Right and Wrong."

RAM Time is an important foundation for family togetherness, security, and problem-solving. If each family member participates with the intent of communicating, the result can be extremely effective. The above guidelines, or suggestions, are general but very effective. They may fit your needs exactly; on the other hand, it is you who must establish the rules and Rituals that fit your environment and needs. If you are seeking a moral and close-knit family (the essence of material wealth and abundance), successful parents have proven that there is nothing more productive than **RAM Time;** it works, and it works well.

In fact, not only does it work well under "normal" conditions, it works even better when things are out of kilter. For example, say a member of the household is unemployed: RAM Time might be an excellent stage to discuss plans and procedures to obtain employment. Also, discussions of what went right and wrong during the previous time span, and how the time could have been better spent, or how the plan could be better implemented or arranged during a future encounter, could be invaluable to successful closure. The marvelous impact is that open discussion presents the possibility of strengthening each member of the unit as well as the entire family.

I know you may be thinking, these kinds of talks should be between the parents only, children should be left out. All I can say is, you are the leader, regardless of what the topic: nothing happens until somebody does something. However, everything starts in the mind: the final decision of how you handle your family's pursuit of happiness starts in your mind, and causes things to happen under your tutelage.

Under any conditions, RAM time relationships produce a closer knit family, a more secure, more successful individual unit: your Little One will soak it up and grow proportionately to your involvement and sharing.

No doubt, RAM Time relates to the immediate inner circle of the family workings; yet, there is more to the family than the immediate inner circle. With that in mind, there is a consistent and worthwhile thought that good/successful parents have agreed is important. The thought: regardless of your position in life, financial or otherwise; always take at least one <u>family-vacation</u> every year: minimum of one week, maximum of two weeks, to do nothing but relax and have fun (together).

If you don't know what to do to relax and have fun, just do anything different than what you have done in the past. By all means, include your Little One in the loop and plans, as if his life depends on it… in many ways, it does. You might say, "That seems like a waste of precious time," and you're right, it does. However, an analogy might be: to insure that he doesn't run out of gas, a driver might want to refuel periodically.

Speaking of refueling, it comes in a variety of forms: some physical, some mental, some spiritual. Refueling also might have a tendency to come at various times of the day: when you awake to a glorious sunrise, or end the day under an incredible sunset. Or maybe you just say a prayer at bedtime to end the day and/or prepare for tomorrow.

Whatever the case, sometimes you just might cause a positive change by welcoming a spiritual aid.

By all means, welcome your Little One within the loop by sharing your belief that there is something beyond life as we know it.

Spiritual Aid

Just as an aside: "Now I lay me down to sleep; I pray to God my soul to keep: if I should die before I wake, I pray to God my soul to take." That's the prayer my sister and I were taught by my mom. Of course, we were young and impressionable, and we were taught to get in the proper praying-position by being on our knees with our palms together and clasped under our chinny chin chins. That was a nightly routine. It was very effective in laying to rest all the trials and tribulations of the day (even though there was a monster in the closet next to my bed).

Atheist will probably say, "That's indoctrination!" True, it is; on the other hand, it provides a foundation of support of a higher power that aids in reducing concerns of safety and security.

In addition, when we add other prayers of support such as a song of David: "The Lord is my shepherd, I shall not want, He makes me lie down in green pastures, He restores my soul; He leads me in the paths of righteousness, for His names sake. Yea, I walk through the valley of the shadow of death, I will fear no evil; for thou art with me; Your rod and Your staff, they comfort me. You prepare a table before me in the presence of my enemies; You anoint my head with oil; my cup runs over. Surely goodness and mercy shall follow me all the days of my life; and I will dwell in the house of the Lord forever," it provides a reassuring inner strength that, when added to physical awareness, is unbeatable.

Remember, we are molding a little stick of dynamite, a being that will make the world his for the taking. He will mold it (the world) into what he wants it to be and adapt his conditions to suit his desires. Many individuals will say, "That's easy for you to say, but how does one do that?" We at the "Bridge to Success" say, it's also easy to do! Keep in mind, you set the stage, and when you treat life in such a way that it (life) is a barrel of fun, at the same time is a serious condition with consequences and alternatives, then you can mold your Little One into all he is meant to be. All you need to do is personalize the technique, method or whatever you want to call it as revealed on this site. Personalize means make it yours, make it fit the uniqueness of you and your child. If you need help, talk to me and relate your concerns via email: parentchild4now@gmail.com.

My mom also taught my sister and me her other favorite song of David: "Make a joyful noise unto the Lord, all ye lands. Serve the Lord with gladness: come before His presence with singing. Know ye the Lord He is God; it is He that has made us and not we ourselves; we are His people, and the sheep of His pasture. Enter into His gates with thanksgiving, and into His courts with praise: be thankful unto Him and bless His name. For the Lord is good, His mercy is everlasting; and His truth endures to all generations." That's a powerful prayer, but it might be meaningless if you, the parent, cannot explain what it means. Well, what does it mean? When your little one asks, "What does, 'make a joyful noise unto the Lord' mean, dad?" what would you say?

You might say, "That's a good question, son: first of all, I'm sure you would agree that you did not make yourself: right? and I think you would also agree that we enjoy being alive: running, jumping, laughing, and surviving the challenges of life: right?." "'Make a joyful noise unto the Lord' means, thank your maker: thank you Lord for providing us with eyes that allow a beautiful sunset to be seen, with a nose that allows us to smell yummy bar-b-queue ribs, with ears that we can hear the music of mom's singing, etc, etc."

That's a good time to illustrate the value of thanking our Creator for what we have, as opposed to concerning ourselves with things we do not have.

Even as we talk, there are those who do not have eyes to see, ears to hear, voices to speak, legs to walk, arms to hug. That might be a good time to talk about Nick Vujicic, an individual who was born without arms, and without legs; nevertheless he is an inspiration to millions of individuals who have all their physical anatomical assets: he is really something. He thanks God for being who he is. He has produced tapes and written books about his belief in the goodness and love of God. You might want to share it with your Little One.

The atheists might say, "There is no God: praying, is a waste of time. Not only that, it's easy for you to talk, but what about those poor individuals in the ghetto, the ones who are afraid of physical and/or mental abuse, the ones that are abused in one manner or another everyday of their lives: what about them?" The answer is, there might be nothing we can do about or for them in our "Bridge to Success." However, when it comes to you and your Little One, you can not only protect him and arm him with the tools he needs to rise above the ghetto (victim) mentality, you can be assured he will never, ever be poor or want for anything an individual can desire or need.

That's the gift you can provide to <u>your</u> Little One and the world. If prayer is not your cup of tea, don't pray; nevertheless, if as a parent, you utilize the methods on this site, your Little One will never, ever be poor.

Please allow me to add one more thing: poor is a mindset, not a condition. An individual can have a ton of material things: houses, cars, clothes, money, etc., and still be poor. At the same time, an individual can be without the finest of material assets and not be poor.

Our "Bridge to Success," part one, sets you up to provide the mindset for your Little One so that he will never, ever be poor. Part two is designed to help guide you and him through the realm of enjoying life as it is meant to be – "a barrel of fun." In other words, Part two is designed to convert our healthy thoughts into positive strength-laden action. That's the real power behind this book. It is designed from the point of view that, all you, the parent, need to do is, "Make it happen and make it fun." That's one of the goals along the path on our "Bridge to Success."

The final step in providing the necessary ingredients in forging ahead and molding your little "Bundle of Joy" into a potent member of our society is to honor his **ancestors**. I say final step; on the other hand, good parents say it is not a step; it is an image that begs to be portrayed all along the path that engenders individual and family power, strength and security.

The image says that we should treat our ancestors beginning with you, the parent, with reverence. Regardless of how inept or magical; how fearlessly we love or hate them, and every point of reference between the two, we should project the idea that grandparents and beyond are the epitome of efficiency, love, and protection.

Many individuals have found that one of the most beneficial ways to honor the ancestors and the ancestral tree is through the establishment and/or active participation in a **family reunion**. If a family reunion is already in place that's excellent: if it's not, now might be the time to begin one; however, to keep a tradition alive, a great deal of work and dedication is required. With the above in mind, many families rotate control every two to five years. Also, a roster of attendees and the method of communicating with each of them, plus a control-aid, listing important recommended road bumps to avoid, and a 1-5 grading of location and dates are provided.

It takes a special person to lead the way, and that person must have a great deal of patience and support to make it happen. On the other hand, the pleasant, and sometimes surprising, point of interest is that practically every family has that one person that can spark the interest, build the momentum, and cause it to happen. You, the parent, can be the one who continues to mold your Little One and further solidify his "Bridge to Success."

During reunion festivities, one item on the agenda might be to plan a special tribute to the most senior member (the oldest) of the family, and the newest member (the youngest).

Some of you might say or think, "That buffoon, no way am I going to place him (or her) on a pedestal for my Little One to emulate!" If that's the way you feel, fine, but keep in mind your motive in developing and molding your Little One is two-fold. First and foremost, you are attempting to mold a little stick of dynamite: one who will maintain or begin a tradition of excellence.

Second, our ancestors should be honored if for no other reason than that they are still alive. Not only are they alive; because of their longevity, they reside in the richest society in the world (in terms of morality as well as material wealth). The objective is to mold a mind and body into an individual who will know he is secure, who will know he is loved, who will know he has the strength and will to maintain, and if not already in place, to begin a tradition of power and excellence.

"But," you say, "What if my parents suffer from substance abuse, people abuse, mental impairment of one kind or another, etc., what should I do then?" No doubt about it, that problem could impact a young life. With your knowledge and prior insight, you will understand that the beneficial effect of treating them as though they are as honorable as you would desire them to be, far outweighs any other treatment. You should demand, by the way you treat them, that your Little One honors them as though they are beyond reproach.

"But why should I do that if they don't deserve it?" On the contrary, they do deserve it; in fact, if that is factual, they deserve it more than the average ancestor. After all is said and done, they have problems because they have unresolved issues. The point is, don't allow their unresolved issues to become your problem.

Remember what we said about the "big three?" First, provide **lots of hugs and kisses** (in this instance, it is extremely short-lived) – those hugs and kisses say "I love you: 'I've got your back.'" That's true, but you also have his front; in other words, at all times you must be vigilant and at the same time not over-protective.

"But how do I know when I am being over-protective?" That's easy: you are being over-protective if you don't allow her to fall; you are being vigilant when you don't allow her to fall from a height too great. You are being over-protective when after she falls you hasten to pick her up before she has the opportunity of picking herself up. You are being vigilant when after she falls, and struggles to get up, you don't allow her to get frustrated. Admittedly, sometimes the line between vigilance and over-protection is not easily defined; nevertheless, keep in mind, there is a difference, it could make a difference in the progress of your Little-One.

When it comes to your ancestors, you are being over-protective when you avoid contact with them; you are being vigilant when you do not allow unsupervised contact with them. You will probably note that we are now overlapping the mental and physical, so let's not do that.

The point is, our ancestors are an important link to the past as well as a promise fulfilled for the future. Family re-unions are not a necessity; nevertheless, the making of America was a gigantic struggle for our ancestors. True, we cannot live our lives for them, nor can they relive their lives for us, but we can forge ahead and help recover the promise of our Founding Fathers when they declared independence for our nation with the words, "We hold these truths to be self-evident…" Only this time, it's the independence of your Little One!

Now is the time to put Part One in perspective: let's recap!

1. The Big Three: Provide
    a) Lot's of talk/listening, and hugs & kisses (expresses love & security)
    b) Lot's of no's (helps set the foundation for self-discipline) – don't forget the Parent's Alternate Phrases to "No" (PAPs)
    c) Limiting foreign objects (helps develop imagination & creativity)
2. The Critical Three: administering the concepts of:
    a) Love (helps develop the image of personal worth)
    b) Sex (expresses the prime emotion that drives physical/mental health)
    c) Money (relates production to true personal material & mental wealth)
3. Fear: Identifies the "Silent spoiler" and reduces its limiting effect.
4. Ram Time: A method of developing individual, and family security and strength.
5. Annual "Fun Time" The value of vacationing as a family (together)
6. Ancestors: The value of honoring ancestral heritage

Please standby for a brief interlude that I call: "Power of the Parent." The things I highlight have little to do with the technique/method of parenting. On the other hand, I thought it important to comment on several issues because the content is of great concern to many parents and non parents alike (especially lil ol me). Hopefully, you will read and absorb my thoughts herein…

Power of the Parent!

If you are a parent or thinking of becoming one, I applaud you; however, don't bask in the applause too quickly because it's easy to be a lousy parent and <u>not</u> know it. I know this to be true because I was one (once a parent; always a parent, lousy or not).

First of all let me say, at first I was going to use a pseudonym as the author of this work: I was not going to identify myself because I am not proud of being a lousy parent. I'm a good person, but I failed miserably in living up to the status of "good parent."

Several reviewers who read the opening of this effort asked two questions; first, "If you are not proud of what you did or failed to do as a parent, why advertise it?" That's an excellent question, the answer is forthcoming; however, before I answer, let's be perfectly clear about what constitutes being a lousy parent. On second thought, let's put it this way: there are two kinds of lousy parents: those who know they are lousy and those who do not. This effort is slanted toward both, but more toward the one like me who doesn't know it.

Every time I see or hear of a youngster who has followed in his parents footsteps, I acknowledge the fact that there stands a good parent. At the same time I acknowledge the fact that I was a lousy parent – that burns me up. I've made tons of poor decisions in my day, but of all those that I look back upon with regret, being a lousy parent tops the list.

I have long ago qualified for Medicare; therefore, I don't have a great deal of time left to make up for my lousiness. It is hoped that this book will help others <u>not</u> step into the pool of regret that I embody. One more thing: a good parent contributes incredible value to society, his family, and himself. If this book accomplishes half of what I intend, it might, to some degree, make up for my parental lousiness, and pay homage to that which parenting embodies. I hope that answers your question, "Why advertise being a lousy parent?"

A lousy parent is not necessarily evil or lazy, he or she is simply one who produces a child but doesn't continually provide the youngster with direction necessary to help in his pursuit of independence and happiness. The result could produce an individual who lacks a productive work ethic, one who suffers from mental and/or physical problems well into adulthood, and maybe even for a lifetime.

On the other hand, a good parent is one whom his/her offspring wants to emulate. The parent can be a saint or sinner, it really doesn't matter. If the child wants to be like his parent(s), then as long as that remains true, the parent has done his job. That's what parenting is all about. Even though that is true, if a child wants to pursue happiness in an altogether different direction than his parent(s), that's not a contradiction. The good parent continues to guide and direct his child toward accomplishing the culmination of his (the child's) desires. Incidentally, a parent doesn't have to be good, he doesn't have to be correct in his premises, decisions, or choices; all he needs to do is provide direction for his child. Then when the child becomes an adult he will feel good about himself and those around him, and he'll be productive without expecting unearned gifts from anyone else or his government.

One more thing: if a parent has many children, it only takes one to satisfy the label "good parent." On the other hand, he can also be a lousy parent to the others (weird, isn't it?).

I mentioned two questions that surfaced among reviewers of this effort, so allow me to address the other one. "If you were such a lousy parent, why should anybody who wants to be a good parent, listen to you?" That's also a legitimate question that demands an answer. The answer is this: I have been a parent since 1971; in looking back, I can see that I started out incredibly parental; however, in the final analysis I ended as a lousy parent. The strange thing is that in the not too distant past, had you asked me if I had been a good parent I would have answered "yes." There is no doubt that there are tons of parents that fit that mold. On the other hand, once the realization hit, it caused me to look deeply into the reasons for that failure. I immediately began to put together a plan to discover what "good parents" do, and what others can do to practically guarantee successful parenthood.

I knew that the most effective plans are those that are simple, not too extensive, and easy to follow. I also knew that to develop such a plan I had to start with me. I simply had to delve into the strength of my limited parenting success and expose the winning ways: at the same time tear apart the weakness of my parenting failure.

The next step was to observe and study other parents and their children in an effort to nail down the essentials of successful parenting. I did that with numerous parents and children. Upon completion of that study, and after reviewing the results and merging them with what experts agree are sound principles, I found that in the overwhelming majority, those who possess the title of "successful parent" have one overriding detail in common. They provide guidance, support, and discipline to their children within a recipe of morality, and they do it throughout all the parent/child stages on the road to independence.

I want desperately to help other individuals avoid the agony I have endured: toward that end I endeavored to develop a successful-parent plan (SPP). Through observation, association, and interviews I discovered the secret, recorded it, synthesized it, and herewith submit it to you. Hopefully, that answers the question, "Why should anybody listen to (me)?"

The dictionary defines "lousy" with words like mean, nasty, contemptible, painful, and unpleasant: I was none of those, but those are the words that come to mind when I view my overall performance as a parent. I am in the twilight of my years; as I look back, I see a dismal parent who failed to provide the parenting essentials necessary to aid his offspring in becoming a productive and caring adult, one who identifies himself as a unique and worthy individual.

Yeh, yeh, yeh, I know what some of you are thinking, because some of you have stated it to me, "You're being too hard on yourself: how about the child, he certainly has some responsibility to himself?" I agree; nevertheless, I see it as an 80/20 concept. Eighty percent of the child's success resides with the parent: the primary key is the first five years of the child's existence. If, during the first five to seven years of the child's existence, the parent uses the methodology outlined within this effort, the child will blossom (regardless of the strength/weakness of his genes, or other influences). The level, degree, or promptness of progress might depend on the gene strength; nevertheless, the "Bridge to Success" method is guaranteed to impact your child enormously.

All that being said; I am proud of the fact that even though I was a lousy parent, I provided the essentials of character, integrity, and caring that is part and parcel of a good individual.

Let me attempt to clarify an important point: A good parent is one who does two things successfully. The first thing is that he causes his child to feel good about himself and those with whom he associates. The complimentary component is that he promotes awareness indicative of becoming a worthy and productive citizen; a person who adds value to himself and his community. Incidentally, the value could be in the form of an athlete, a professor, a mobster, a truck driver, a politician, a model; again, it doesn't matter. Keep in mind now: being a good citizen and being a good parent may be entirely two different things.

Sometimes a person looks at his past and savors the good times: he says to himself, "Well done". That produces a good feeling. On the other hand, sometimes a person looks at his past and knows that he failed to live up to the expectations of his station in life. The station of a parent is a challenging one to behold: we should thank and celebrate the good ones – by the way, invite me to the celebration; I promise I won't tell anybody _you_ invited me.

Incidentally, I realize you may be thinking, "His children must be in prison, dead, performed a dastardly deed, or something terrible for him to call himself a 'lousy parent.'" Not so, as you will note in my Dedication Appendix F, that is not the case. However, had I had the knowledge that I bring forward in this book, they would have had a much greater span of time and level of success in their pursuit of happiness.

To continue: The content of this book is a guide for establishing an effective and joyous parent/child relationship. Many parents who have read it say they wish they had possessed this as a guide when they started, and had the good fortune to digest it. Readers have advanced the idea that the marvelous thing about this book is that whether the parent/child is male or female, single or married, heterosexual or not, it is equally effective. Also, ethnic, religious, or national origin differences do not matter.

That being said, it is important to note that most individuals believe the **optimal relationship** is for the care-givers to be of a male and female partnership. In each instance caregivers can teach a young one how to <u>act</u> like a male/female, but not how to <u>be</u> an adult male/female. The reason this is important is that the influence of the opposite gender and how one interrelates with the other, is of prime importance in the development of a healthy and well balanced individual. Arguments to the contrary cannot refute that fact. I won't invest the time here, debating the truth/fallacy of that statement.

During the past few years, controversy has risen because of the emergence of same-sex marriages. I am not opposed to homosexual activity, it is simply a physical response to natural pleasurable urgings of a person's anatomy: the urge is natural, the response is not. I do not oppose homosexual activity; however, I am unconditionally opposed to same-sex marriage under **any** conditions.

On the other hand, the jury is still out regarding the health and welfare of a child of abusive parents, single parents, and same-sex parents on the one hand, and love and discipline on the other. In addition, when it comes to the parents, a person need not utter marriage vows in order to possess a durable relationship; however, it might be important to the family that the parents are committed in such a way that marriage is a legal bind that says they will be there for the child forever. I know you may be thinking that is in conflict with my previous statement, so please allow me to say it again.

I am unconditionally opposed to same-sex marriage under any conditions!

The above is merely a preamble to part two of the work of this book. Taken in total, there is no need to be alarmed that my comments may be counter to traditional belief; it's just that regardless of where an individual stands, the essentials of parenting outlined within these pages are "right-on." As one can imagine, being a parent is a complex issue, and demands direct and caring effort. On the other hand, it can be easy and fun. All you need are two attributes: total honesty and the desire to share yourself with your Little One.

Now here is the part that is so very difficult and disheartening. Because our society is so confused when it comes to careful and protective treatment on the one hand, and doing what is needed to educate and communicate with our little ones on the other; somebody with a dirty/evil mind is going to be over-protective to the point of nausea, and claim child abuse, child pornography, child neglect, etc. The problem is, some well-meaning individuals (social worker, neighbor, innocent observer) are prone to place themselves in the position of "protector" -- "Call the authorities, something should be done about this!"

Well, damn, damn, and double damn, our disjointed society and local authorities have placed us in the position where a parent is afraid to properly perform her parental obligations without being looked upon as a pervert (the state of Delaware is a prime example: it's illegal for a parent to spank her child). On the other hand in an extremely tiny percentage of cases, it's true, the individual is a pervert. So, what are we to do? Remember back in chapter four, we talked about the "silent spoiler" (FEAR)? Read it again, identify what it is, then repeat the key -- "Here is the key that will disable the frightening effects of fear:" This is what you, the parent, must impart to your Little One: "When a person does that which is moral and couples it with producing the best that is within him, there is absolutely nothing to fear, **<u>ever</u>**." The same applies to you, the parent!

Delaware is the only state in the union that has deemed spanking to be illegal; HELP!

Remember when we talked about vigilance and being over-protective? Remember that? We all hope there is never a need to use "corporal punishment" on our little "Bundle of Joy." Just to highlight the difference: we are being vigilant when we do not allow a parent to beat his Little One to a pulp; on the other hand, we are being over-protective when we attempt to stop a parent from spanking her Little One.

"Well doggone it, what must we do?" I say, society should place parents on a higher authority-level than the local or national authorities. When we find a parent or group of parents, who have violated the parenting code (beyond a shadow of doubt), the offender should be treated more harshly than violations of other offenses. On the other hand, parents should have much greater latitude in disciplining their offspring than is now allowed. It is believed that this book will provide a wealth of ammunition that includes obviating "corporal punishment."

I want to add the idea that there is never a need to punish a child, maybe it's a matter of semantics, but punishment is not part of successful parenting. On the other hand, pain (not injury) is part of **corporal persuasion**: the natural inclination of all of us is to seek pleasure and avoid pain. The effective parent judiciously uses methods to utilize nature's automatic tendency of all of us. You've probably overheard your elders proclaim "Return us to the good 'ol days where we looked out for each other without being a turd!" [(I looked this up in my dictionary to be sure I spelled it right: not there! If I spelled it correctly, good: if not, let me be clear: I mean "obnoxious," (I like "turd" better)].

How many times have you heard the statement, "Being a parent is no cup of tea: it's tough. Wouldn't it be great if an operating manual came with every child"? Yes, I guess it would, but it sure wouldn't be as much fun, and we sure wouldn't derive as much internal satisfaction (this book provides an exception). What makes it so tough is that every child is different from every other child, even if he or she is a twin or any multiple; he is different in temperament, mentality, disposition, and alertness from every other child. In addition, all parents also differ in those same essentials, plus they respond differently to differences among their offspring. Largely, children develop in various ways based on the parent's input (even more than the economic or cultural environment surrounding them).

Regardless of input, parents have a humongous role in guiding their children and molding our society: whether they agree or not, they are role-models for their children. Being a role-model is always an ultra important responsibility; however, the rewards of successful parenting are unmatched by any other endeavor.

Good parents are builders of strong, productive individuals, and strong, productive individuals build strong societies. If being a "good parent" is your goal, you have come to the right place. One of the pluses of this book is that it can be read in just a few hours; however, the primary plus is two-fold: first, the fundamental problems that every parent faces is properly identified and consumed; second, parents will find a wealth of easy and common-sense ways to help infants, toddlers, and preschoolers develop a love of life, a love of learning, and a moral foundation that lasts a lifetime. An exciting addition is that handled properly, the issues outlined within these pages can be extended to be effective through the pre-teen years and beyond.

The title of this work was established to support the idea that an individual need not be a bad or abusive person to be a lousy parent. In fact, a person can be a good, law-abiding individual and still be a lousy parent – I am living proof of that statement. Beyond the title is the ever-present objective: identify the essentials of good parenting and take action to make changes in the lives of all of us. Remember, change starts with "me."

I am one of many parents who possess an outlook that says children are our most valuable asset; however, we don't own them, we are simply caretakers. On the other hand, we need to be more than caretakers; we need to be construction workers. Our mission should be to mold a child's inner foundation to the degree that our fledgling Little One will possess the necessary tools that will motivate him to be the best he can be. Many reviewers say in this work, "Bridge to Success," we have done that extremely well.

My goal in writing this book is to aid every individual in the art of being a "good/successful parent." That's the key: we can look to government, groups, friends and neighbors, but when the smoke has cleared, it's a matter of one-on-one – you and your little "Bundle of Joy."

We have been told that selfishness, feelings, and needs are automatic, that's true; however, not so with Love and Discipline. Think about it: the newborn observes the world and people around him with awe and admiration. The simple reason is that the rest of us can do things that in his wildest dreams he would love to do, but can't.

Findings indicate that parental love from a newborn is practically automatic and fairly easy to maintain. On the other hand, discipline is easy only if the disciplinarian mixes it with healthy doses of love, and even then, discipline can be a difficult matter to perform. Love can easily be nurtured, effective Discipline must be practiced. This work was approached from the standpoint that a proper beginning makes it much easier to embrace both Love and Discipline at a high level of intensity.

Whatever the case, we welcome you to the world of parenting. It may be different from many others you will find, probably because it is counter to the established norm of such books. Parenting is a particularly selfish endeavor, yet it is extremely rewarding. You have probably heard the phrase "make love." That's a misnomer, a person can't "make love." However, we can supplement and integrate the makings of Love into our daily activity and cause a response the same as a lover: that's what we do here.

Many reviewers believe you will find this book to be the treasure that you, the parent, have been seeking; however, as my aunt Dot used to say, "The proof of the pudding is in the eating." In other words, read it: if you find it absorbing, great: if not, put it down and find another. Either way, write me (child4now@gmail.com) and let me know your thoughts.

Before I end this part one, let me say that it is with great appreciation that I acknowledge **World Book, Inc**. for their high quality, yet most readable educational material. They produce extraordinarily supportive products to aid in the growth and development of our youth. In fact, part two of this work was inspired by the content of their little booklet titled, "The First Five Years: Little Beginnings (Starting your child on a lifetime of learning)." Unfortunately, the little booklet is no longer in print; however, **I thank them for permission to use it** as a guidebook for part two of this work.

So much for part one.

I don't want to get ahead of myself, but you can obtain a preview of what you can expect to accomplish in Part Two of this work by viewing Appendix A, "Checklist of progress: Can your Little One recognize and identify…" (see Appendix A)

APPENDIX A

Checklist of Progress

Can your Little One recognize and identify:

- ☐ Basic colors: <u>red</u>, <u>yellow</u>, <u>blue</u>, <u>orange</u>, <u>green</u>, and <u>purple</u>.
- ☐ Basic shapes: <u>circles</u>, <u>squares</u>, <u>triangles</u>, <u>rectangles</u>.
- ☐ <u>Big and small</u> (elephant & mouse),
- ☐ <u>Long and short</u> (horizontal – <u>side to side</u>)
- ☐ <u>Tall and short</u> (vertical – <u>up and down</u>)

Position, direction, time, and order, are things that most of us can't even remember learning. If children aren't aware of them when they begin school they will learn soon. If it is experienced as pleasure, the love of learning becomes much easier to acquire. It is you who provides your Little One with a head start; you will earn his confidence in you and knowledge that he can depend on you.

Throughout Part Two (one to five years), we talk about working with him to help him understand positions such as:

- ☐ **up and down,**
- ☐ **in and out,**
- ☐ **front and back,**
- ☐ **over and under,**
- ☐ **top and bottom.**

Also understanding

- ☐ **hot and cold**,
- ☐ **fast and slow**,

and have a sense of time: know

- ☐ **night from day** and
- ☐ **the seasons**. Plus we talk about him knowing
- ☐ his own **age** and
- ☐ his **birthday**.

Finally, we talk about working with him so he will be able to:

- ☐ **retell simple stories** in order; for example, in the story of the three little pigs, he will be able to tell which house the Big Bad Wolf blows down first.
Talking, listening, and **observing** are skills children use to get ready to read and write.

Schoolrooms are filled with **letters, words**, and **language** activities. Reinforcing these activities at home helps children as well as their teachers. Follow my lead, and your Little One will be able to do the following:

- ☐ Recognize alphabet letters
- ☐ remember objects from a picture
- ☐ Know some nursery rhymes
- ☐ know parts of the body
- ☐ Follow simple directions
- ☐ know common household objects and how they are used
- ☐ Identify common zoo animals
- ☐ listen politely to adults and other children
- ☐ Recognize common sounds such as, bird songs, car horns, trains, sirens, etc.
- ☐ Talk in sentences
- ☐ pronounce her own first and last names

☐ Identify his own written first name
☐ identify other children by name
☐ complete a sentence with
☐ pretend to read and write (scribbling) the correct words
☐ like having books and have favorite stories
☐ answer questions about a short story
☐ tell the meaning of simple words heard in a story
☐ look at pictures and tell a story

The wonderful thing is that you will be, and remain, his hero (role-model) for the rest of his life, and both of you will enjoy an enduring, successful, and fascinating world that you and he created together to enjoy.

Your Little One will learn many things from you because learning essentials are part of everyone's existence, especially around the home. As you note the environs, <u>talk</u> about them; point out differences so that she will understand:

1) Basic colors: <u>red, yellow, blue, orange, green</u>, and <u>purple</u>.
2) Basic shapes: <u>circles, squares, triangles</u> and <u>rectangles</u>.
3) <u>Big and small</u> (elephant & mouse),
4) <u>Long and wide</u> (horizontal – <u>side to side</u>)
5) <u>Tall and short</u> (vertical – <u>up and down</u>)

Position, direction, time, and order, are things that most of us can't even remember learning. Just introducing and critically playing games with the face of an <u>analog clock</u> will help develop instantaneous awareness of the actual time, help aid in understanding direction, maps, the circle, etc. Also, I firmly encourage playing card games with your Little One: games where the numbers and other marks are exhibited (one favorite that you might consider is "Uno," where the use of colors and numbers make it fun for all ages). The objective is to help your little "Bundle of Joy" learn to visualize numbers and arrangement; the result is that simple math becomes simpler.

Of course, if children aren't aware of these primary issues it is not a big deal because when they begin school they will soon learn. On the other hand, the "games" you play at home will provide her with a head start and motivate her to make learning fun. The point is, the love of learning will become much easier to acquire if you provide her with a head start.

Often, caregivers shudder with apprehension to think that their Little One might ask questions they cannot answer: the feeling should be just the opposite. You should see any and all inquiries as times you can use to lead her in finding answers in an enjoyable manner, plus, she will have greater confidence in you. In addition, she will know that the things you tell her are accurate and she can depend upon them.

This brings us to the attention of using ***teachable moments***: you will have tons of them. However, if you are like most of us, you'll miss a bunch; on the other hand, when you courageously complete one, it might bring tears to your eyes and a smile to your innards. Whenever possible, try to recognize and take advantage of every one of them. (That's Gervaise, "talking" with my friend, Robert Hinkle)

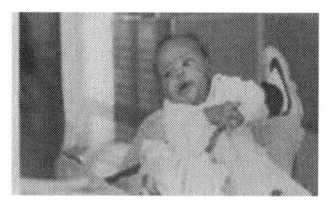

The best and most effective way to do that is to latch on to anything that your Little One enjoys doing and do it with her. The long term advantage of that is you can, just by talking during a game, brush upon the moral things to do, and easily identify the right people with whom to associate, etc. I know, I know, it's easier said than done, but believe me, it not only is well worth the effort, it will pay long term dividends.

Always teach things that support integrity, character, and the will to win. Hammer home the fact that cheaters never win, that anything worthwhile has a price, and that the price of consistent winning is an irreplaceable product of practice, practice, practice.

Teach vision, planning and goal-setting, and caress the attributes of patience and pride. Be careful though, don't present a classroom-setting type teaching: I know that's easier said than done, the easiest and most productive way to do it is make it part of your life. Remember, games are thumbnail sketches of life without stress: take advantage of them (games)!

Newsworthy pieces in the media offer many chances to illustrate everything of value. Use reading-matter as a relaxing and informative teaching tool, limit television viewing (alone) severely, primarily because it inhibits the imagination to an astonishing degree.

Use the LIBRARY often when you and/or your Little One have questions: remember, part of your wisdom is knowing when and where to seek answers to questions and problems. The great thing is that you and he will share the method of problem-solving <u>together</u>: that is priceless.

APPENDIX B

What to do to guide your little one to...

Part Two, <u>section one</u> embraces the first year. During that year, a foundation can be erected that will provide a core to support all the challenges that life has to offer.

I have highlighted some of the simple and uncomplicated things a parent (or caregiver) can do when she thinks, "What can I do to help my little one...?" Or maybe you know someone who fits that description: you can help without appearing nosy or prying. The following appendix is offered as a mini reference point:

Adjust: Adjust to his/her new world	(Page 98)
Body (know and enjoy): Explore the body	(Page 107)
Create: Be more creative	(Page 102)
Accept Critique: critique your little one	(Page 104)
Stop Crying: I.D and solve the problem when he cries	(Page 94)
Recognize and accept Encouragement: to encourage him	(Page 103)
Have more Energy: Energize each hour of each day	(Page 95)
Be Friendly: Get used to interacting with other people	(Page 93)
Help others: encourage him to help around the house	(Page 105)

Promote life-skills: most important skill for her to master	(Page 95)
Develop personality: life in her personality and manner	(Page 97)
Develop Reading skills: motivate him to want to read	(Page 106)
Be relaxed and Caring: teach rhythm, music, love and caring	(Page 132)
Obey Rules of society: start establishing rules of behavior	(Page 112)
Learn a Practical Sport: Learn the most practical sport in life	(Page 95)
Be aware of Safety: be safe around water	(Page 95)
Become Secure: Learn about love and security	(Page 93)
Learn to listen and Talk: Learn to talk	(Page 93)
Become Worldly: Learn about the world around him	(Page 93)
Use of Time: provide quality time	(Page 100)
Establish daily routines: naptime, bedtime, etc	(Page 98)
..........Improve his physical skills Provide a plaything	(Page 125)

PART TWO

If you have not read Part One of this effort, then you are somewhat at a disadvantage. The reason I say that is because part one covers the mental and moral preparation on the road to being a good parent. One way or another, the parent(s) molds the child and prepares him to address the challenges of life. Preparation is the foundation that acknowledges life as a two-stage affair: the mental and the physical.

We highlighted the fact that all things begin with thought, but nothing happens until we do something. That's why this book is a two-stage affair. A parent is like a battery in an automobile, he or she provides the spark to start that engine. A "**good/successful** parent" does more than that. He/she provides support, guidance and direction through the stages of parent/child relationship to the point of the child's independence (and beyond).

The first year of the interaction between the caregiver and his Little One is undeniably the key to success and happiness of the new arrival. That is undoubtedly the most influential year of a person's life. In that section, our guiding comments are intended to be simple and uncomplicated and I think they are. The same applies to the next section, the only difference is that in that section you and he (your child) are taken from the end of the first year to the end of year five – generally, right before he enters formal schooling. I call it "The Final Four."

Since passion is the mother of invention, and repetition is the mother of skill and foundation of habit, let me repeat a previous statement. This book is about guiding your Little One, and helping develop him to do and be the best he can be. The **inclination** to do what is right; that is, to be a morally upright human being, is fashioned during the first few years **prior** to entering formal schooling; in fact, that is true even before emergence from the mother's womb. The development of a human being with a conscience, with a will to do right by himself and others, is largely a matter of building a moral foundation, and teaching your child to appreciate and enjoy being alive. That's what this book is about – the simple and uncomplicated joy of being alive (through the eyes of the parent/child relationship).

I was motivated to write this book because the learning that takes place **before** children start school sets the stage for everything they learn **in** school, and in **life**. That's why the parent is his child's first and most important teacher. If we do it right, the result will last a lifetime and friends, neighbors and countrymen will gain immense pleasure and success because of it.

A child who is happy and who feels secure, is a child who will **choose** to develop the moral character that will propel him to heights of accomplishments that he was created to achieve.

One more thing worth repeating: the contents of this book relates to the treatment of the child, regardless of whether the parent/child is male or female, the parent single or married, heterosexual or not. Ethnic, religious, or national origin differences do not matter. However, the **optimum relationship** is for the caregiver to be a male and female partnership, committed in such a way that marriage is a legal bind that says they will be there for the child forever. Many of us truly believe that a committed relationship between a man and woman is an important link for a durable and moral society.

Let us not linger any longer; we'll simply slide into the meat of this joyous undertaking.

Again, the following effort is <u>not</u> intended to be all-inclusive or in depth; however, it <u>is</u> intended to be very, very helpful and at the same time, simple and uncomplicated. We think you'll see your little "Bundle of Joy" a little differently and with eyes that light up with the joy of parenthood.

/ PART TWO

SECTION ONE

CHAPTER ONE

From Birth to Six Months

The thing that makes it so easy to be a good parent is that from his emergence into our world, your little "**Bundle of Joy**" is **totally** dependent on you for his survival and pleasure. When you carry him out-and-about among the world, be proud of the fact that you are responsible for being a caregiver and molder of a new arrival. Don't be afraid to show him off to friends and strangers alike: in fact, smile and revel in it; it will cause you and him to feel that he is something special and meaningful to you and the rest of the world – and he is.

Meanwhile, you will share and understand that he is adoringly <u>observing</u> your ability to do things that he can only hope one day he can do: simple things such as <u>sitting</u>, <u>standing</u>, and then <u>walking</u>, <u>running</u>, and <u>tumbling</u>. He doesn't know it yet, but you know one day he will be able to talk, walk, and be as physically adjusted as you; maybe even more so. In the meantime your adoring Little One will do anything you say (that's why it is easy to be a successful parent) because, at first, **you are his Superman and he wants to be just like you**.

Just as an aside: an extremely small percentage of infants will not develop as nature intended, either mentally, physically, or both. It could be the result of his gene pool, an accident, foreign bodies ingested in the mother's system, etc. Nevertheless, that's past history, what you do now is what's important. If you are a parent or caregiver of such a child your Little One will require greater time/effort and support than other parents. Just keep in mind that the opening statement of the Declaration of Independence is absolutely true, "We hold these truths to be self-evident, that all (individuals) are created equal…"

That means this book is intended to aid you, the parent, in molding a new society, and regardless of his development, it includes your little "Bundle of Joy." However, also keep in mind, the two critical essentials should be strongly accented: Love & Discipline. Love is easy, discipline can be and usually is difficult – regardless of your Little One's development, you can be confident that use of this book as your guide, plus your caring instincts, will provide positive and lasting results. The difference is, greater discipline and greater patience are required of you; sometimes we don't realize it, but he wants the same things that you want.

It'll be tougher for you than most other parents; on the other hand, when you blanket discipline and all that you do, with a foundation of love, the results will probably astonish you.

To continue: One of the principle keys to parenting success is to treat your Little One with **respect and kindness, along with love and discipline**, as though she really is as important as she is. Never say "Shut up," and never, ever strike her in anger. If you do it right, you may often have the need to say "No," however, you should never accept the need to be negative (develop and become proficient with the use of PAPs).

Have you ever heard a parent say to his adoring Little One, "Say **hello** to the man, son!" And what does he do?

He says, "**Hello!**"

The goal of a parent is to be a good teacher: to teach your Little One how to be a person that brings joy and satisfaction to the world, to you the parent, and to himself.

The fact is, from the moment your child enters our real world of pleasure and happiness, and pain and sorrow, until the time he takes his final breath, you are the first and most influential teacher he will ever have. That will be true even before he brings home that first report card from school.

He will be seeking your approval and admiration. Actually, just between you and me, the precious little secret is that he is seeking two things. First he wants to prove to you that everything you attempted to teach him was not wasted, and second, he wants to prove that he's a hotshot and he is smart enough to pick up on input from other teachers as well as you.

Let's take a look at the first six months of your Little One's life. At first, he may seem to require only milk, sleep, and diapers; however, to grow, he needs more than that.

To learn to talk, he needs to be talked to. Talk to him, no baby talk: talk as though you are talking to a close friend. It doesn't matter what you talk about; in fact, it doesn't have to be meaningful at first, but try to make it meaningful to some degree; for example, "Do you want to take a nap?" "Want to go for a walk" "Want to get a bite to eat" "Let's go see a movie" – the key here is, whatever you say, always make it positive.

At that point it really doesn't matter what you say, he wouldn't get the message anyhow. Having been one with his mom for nine months, he doesn't know where he ends and the rest of the world begins. In fact, he doesn't even know he's a person.

Long before he understands words, he gathers generalized impressions about himself from how he is treated

To learn about love and security, he needs to be cuddled and gently cared for. Remember what we said earlier: give him lots of hugs and kisses. Your little one is a sponge, he is observing everything you do and say. With that in mind, it is paramount that you and your significant other treat each other with caring and affection. It's not "Big Brother" watching, it's your little "Bundle of Joy" watching, and he is watching very carefully.

To learn about the world around him, he needs to see, hear, smell, and touch things and people: especially people. Be careful, don't be **overly** friendly; however, do be friendly to the point of carefully allowing others (whom you trust) to hold him, hug him, and talk to him.

The one thing your little one **never needs** is punishment. If he cries, it is for a reason. He is either uncomfortable (in pain, hungry or afraid), or he wants attention. So, when your child cries, here is a simple approach to identifying and solving the problem:

1) **Check** to be sure he is comfortable -- **No** wet or mushy **diapers** because of urine or bowels.
    a) No pins, needles or other objects **jabbing the skin.**
    b) No illness (check temperature). If high temperature is detected, check your medical manual, and/or call the doctor.
2) Regardless of the situation, gently grab your little "Bundle of Joy" and
3) hug and kiss him, then look him in the eyes and tell him sincerely that you love him. Hug him again and sway him gently. **Check** to see if he is hungry. **Give** the little one a bottle (when possible, the caregiver should **hold the little one and speak to him in subdued tones** while holding the bottle). When appropriate, place him on the breast and let him nibble (breast milk is best, it does two things: it feeds the child essential physical nourishment, some of which cannot be obtained any other way, and it helps cement a special bond between him and you). Continue to Talk to him and sing him a song. You don't have to be a good singer, and it doesn't matter what song you sing but you'll be surprised how you and your child respond to your singing. One of my favorites is the Mother Goose Nursery rhyme: "Rock-a-bye baby on the tree top when the wind blows the cradle will rock... "

As you sing, smile and think about the words you use.

Your child will seldom continue to cry after the above steps have been completed. On the other hand, if after completing them, about **fifteen minutes pass** and your child continues to cry, then place her in a relaxed and safe sleeping position and **let her continue to cry**. The chances are great, **she will simply cry herself to sleep**, and she will have pleasant feelings as she drifts into la la land.

The above is a cut-and-dried formula that works almost every time. Keep in mind now, nearly all babies cry from time to time. Of course, some cry more than others, but don't blame your baby or yourself; you both deserve kind and loving treatment. However, caring for your child takes patience and energy. That means you should take good care of yourself, take vitamin supplements (usually necessary), and try to get plenty of rest: you'll need it. Also, any time <u>someone you trust</u> volunteers to help, by all means graciously accept the offer.

A word of caution: the one thing you **seldom want** to do (if ever) is over-indulge your Little One, but that's a tough one because you are her super-protector as well as her teacher. The reason is, **over-indulgence usually renders either abuse or spoilage**, and you don't want either. In other words try not to be over-protective. Most babies are naturally cautious; on the other hand, they are also naturally extremely curious, so keep an eye on them at all times, especially around water. If you don't already know how to swim, take swimming lessons.

Whether you do or not, by all means, insure that your little one is taught to swim even before he can walk (it's much easier that way). A YMCA near you can provide classes or information for lessons (it is probably the most practical sport in life: it's fun too!).

An important point to keep in mind is babies are particular sensitive to your emotional state. Strangely, when you are hurried or tense, he is inclined to be fussy and uncooperative when you attempt to feed him or change his diapers. On the other hand, when you appear to be relaxed and have time to bond with him, he's peaceful and quiet as a lamb. Sometimes it might seem like a conspiracy; not so, he's just responding to your body language. It tells him whether the atmosphere is fair or foul.

Now, here are some recommended ideas that you might consider: all children need to feel secure, and love helps them feel that way. With that in mind, give your Little One lots of hugs, kisses and smiles; however, **don't be too liberal with the phrase, "I love you," it should be**

special. In other words, don't just say the words, it is important to **show** that you mean them: the little hugs and kisses reinforce that fact.

It doesn't matter how cranky or ornery you or others think you sound, **your little one loves to hear your voice.** It's soothing and reassuring to him, so talk to him often. **Use his name and look into his eyes as you talk**, and watch his face light up. Also -- **Talk to him as though he is a normal adult.** Ask him questions even though you know you won't get a "real" answer; nevertheless, ask anyway – whatever comes to mind; for instance, "Do you need a clean diaper?" "Do you want to sing along with me?" "Would you like to go for a walk in the park?" "What would you like to eat from the refrigerator?"

On the other hand, **whenever he babbles, talk back to him with the same sounds he uses.** Then introduce new sounds and as he reacts to the new ones you introduce, **repeat the sounds he seems to like best**.

Obtain Mother Goose books from the library: **Read** nursery rhymes and **sing songs** to him. They prepare him to enjoy reading and storytelling. The best nursery rhymes are the one's where you involve his senses: "Patty cake" is a good one, maybe it has been a while, or maybe your caretaker never played it with you, so as a reminder here is how it goes:

Grab the infant by the wrists, look him in the eyes with your loving smile and as you gently smack the infant's palms together say, Patty cake, (smack them together again) patty cake, (smack them together again) baker's man, (smack them together again) make me a cake as fast as you can,

When he babbles, stop and listen to him until he stops, then continue with the rhyme or song. Later, you and he will sing along together, but generally not at that exact time.

Another one of the favorites of the little ones is "Peek-a-boo." That one is simply a matter of covering your face with both hands while peeking between the fingers as if he can't see you, and all of a sudden pull your hands away and say "Peek-a-boo." Be sure to produce a big smile when you do it: kids love that one.

When you and he are out-and-about (if in a car, make sure he is properly protected with a seat belt) **tell him about the things you see and insure he gets to look around**. Also be sure you **talk to him as well as other people** along the way. This way he'll become more secure, more positive, and more persuasive in his personality and mannerisms. **Help him get used to all manner of people: friends,** baby sitters, other family members, store clerks. Don't go overboard, but don't shy away from allowing other people (that you trust) to hold him, starting with just a few minutes at a time.

Cleanliness and safety are always important concerns because illness and injury are reduced that way: make sure everything is clean and safe. When thinking safety you've got to be in a different mindset to insure his safety. Even though we know that the habit of brushing one's teeth is important, the toothbrush, if used improperly, could present a hazard to your little one. No need to be paranoid about it; nevertheless, you have to **think about things that have sharp edges**, things that might **cut or puncture**, things that might **break**, or that might be **swallowed**.

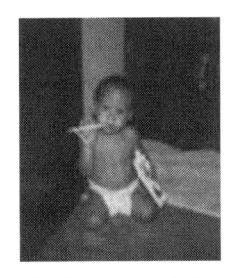

Be careful, consider the potential hazard of **long cords** that he **might get tangled in**; also, be very aware of **small pieces** that might cause **choking**.

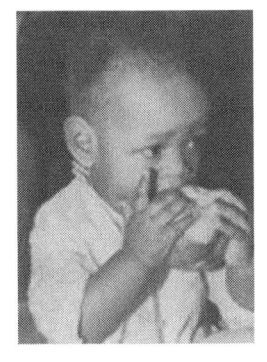

Give her interesting things to look at and touch; for example, a piece of fruit (such as an apple) could serve multiple purposes. You could talk about the color, the shape, the weight, the texture, the fact that it has protective skin, that it can be eaten, that the taste is sweet, that it is nutritious, that it has a stem, which means it grows on trees, etc.

Oftentimes she wants you to know she wants your personal attention; that could be one of the reasons for crying, or an equivalent tantrum. Remember, a good **parent maintains** control at all times; which means, don't fall for any tantrum-like mannerisms. We know you can't always provide personal attention; however, temporary involvement that titillates her imagination is a satisfactory substitute. Consider some of those hanging things above her crib (they call them "mobiles"), as a temporary pacifier and attention-getter. Word of caution: be sure a mobile is out of reach because it can be dangerous if she can reach them from her crib. Provide different sizes, shapes, and colors in as many different places as possible for her to view. Incidentally, television is an excellent medium of exchange; however, it is not a substitute for you, it is best used <u>with</u> you, not instead of you.

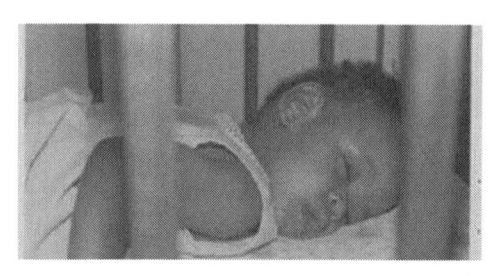

Meanwhile, try to establish routines early on, they help her adjust to her new world. As she grows, schedules and routines become even more important. **Establish a set time for** her **meals**, her **bedtime**, **naps**, and other daily activities.

Jeanne Murphy provides excellent examples of schedules in her book titled, "Baby Tips: Baby's First Year," published by Three Rivers Press.

I know it's not always feasible; however, when you can, as soon as sleeping time is over, get your Little One out of the crib so you can enjoy each other's companionship, and so she can listen and learn from you. Also, be sure to take her with you as often as feasible so you can show her off (she loves it when you show others how much she means to you), and so you can continue to enjoy each other's company. That way she can learn a great deal by watching and listening to you live your life. The important thing is to **have fun with her**, and let her know that you and she are best friends. Again, Word of caution: as a parent, your goal is to be a guide and teacher, you want to mold and guide her to be the best she can be, not a friend (that is simply "icing on the cake"). When you do it right, you will have no concern about the cake or the icing.

At this point, one thing I might share with you is the premier toy a parent can utilize to help develop your child's physical abilities: a ball! A ball can be used as the toy of the ages: it's a primer for teaching throwing and catching. In Appendix E, I reveal the teaching method of the inestimably value of the game of "catch". That's the game that practically obviates the need to respond to your child when/if he says, "I'm bored, there's nothing to do!"

Incidentally, you'll know when to introduce a ball by listening to your instincts. If you have doubts, probably the optimum time is as soon as he is proud of himself because he finally can sit up (yep, he finally did it; isn't it a joy just watching the natural development of your little "Bundle of Joy").

A ball, of all things, can help increase his development and manual dexterity. At the same time, it can allow you to reduce the time it takes to insure your Little One is developing physically. In addition, the ball is not just a toy, it's a tool the parent can use to measure a child's attitude, increase the bonding issue, help him be interactive with other children, and a ton of other positive things. It is so important a tool that in Appendix E, I guide you along the steps of teaching throwing, catching, and how to play catch. Also, I've added a note re game variations.

Take a look, I think you'll appreciate an incredibly useful tool of parenting. Again, it resides in Appendix E.

Now, we have talked about the positive ingredients in a parent/child relationship during the first six months, but we have not talked about some of the potential problems inherent in being a parent, guardian or caretaker of your and our most precious asset. So, let us briefly do that.

Once your Little One understands words, a new avenue aiding his identity to begin to open up. Keep in mind, words have power, but how you use them is the key, that's why the efficient use of PAPs is an important tool in your arsenal.

We'll talk more about critiquing your Little One's behavior later.

At this point, even though RAM Time should become practically automatic, we have not talked about **morality** – the reason for that is that the art of you and your child getting to **know each other** is the primary concern at this stage. Unless your little one gains trust and confidence in you, she will be inclined to stray from the straight and narrow at the faintest tremor of immorality: that is why RAM Time is so important, but don't worry, we'll get there. Meanwhile, a point of interest: she could have been aborted; such was not the case. Either because of **morality**, **reason**, or **fear** she is a presence in your life; which means, the first hurdle is behind you. No need to linger with that fact, it simply means that now **you have an obligation** to secure a human life and provide her the opportunity to be an independent and productive member of our world.

The second item on our agenda is for us to understand that **we do not own our children**. We are simply caretakers entrusted to guide and help develop a fledgling newcomer into a polished adult: one who will further enrich our society and become a positive force in the advancement of our kind (homo sapiens). A polished adult is defined as a productive person, one who respects herself and others, as well as her property and that of others.

The third item on our agenda is for you, the parent, to understand that guiding and helping develop our youthful newcomer is not a matter of time as much as a matter of caring and giving of one's self. **Quality of time is much more important than quantity of time**. In other words, giving of ourselves does not mean a day is more important than an hour, nor does it mean giving material things represents caring and concern. What it does mean is that an hour of caring and sharing of one's self can equal many days, even months, of simply accompanying your child in body alone. I said all that to say that many caregivers contend that there is simply not enough time in the day to do all that needs to be done, plus properly attend to their dependent little ones: not true.

There is no denying that time is a commodity that cannot be replaced -- once gone, it cannot be retrieved. Nevertheless, there are things that you can do to energize each hour of each day and get the most out of what your life has to offer. The single most effective thing you can do is to __plan__ what you are going to do a day (or longer) in advance. The more detailed the plan, the more effective it will be and the more time you will appear to have at your disposal. In addition to that, the greater the time span from beginning to activation of your encounter, the easier it will be to fine tune it. That, in itself, will help you zero in on each individual event of the day. Then when you meet and greet your Little One, you can temporarily wipe everything else out of your mind and devote your total energies to enjoying the alliance with her. Isn't the thought of that exciting?

Remember your favorite love song? Think about those words and respond in kind with your little one (one of my favorites is "Close to You" by the Carpenters).

"*Why* do birds suddenly appear
Every time you are near?
Just like me, they long to be.
Close to you!
Why do stars fall down from the sky,
Every time you walk by?
Just like me,
they long to be
Close to you"

I simply love the thought of those words! Aren't they supreme?

One other thing a person can do: **get organized**; of course, that is easier said than done, but Stephanie Winston has written a book titled, "Getting Organized," it is outstanding and can be a tremendous help. If that one doesn't float your boat, find another one that does aid you in getting organized: organization is one of the keys to help you properly prioritize and remember important activities; in addition, it aids in maintaining punctuality.

There are many other things you can do to maximize your time, but that objective is for some other book not this one.

Finally, the matter of finances comes into play. We talked about the mentality in part one, now comes the action. The strange thing in this matter is that the ability to buy material objects tends to muddy the focus of sharing and caring to the degree that a person often provides his little "Bundle of Joy" with material gifts as opposed to gifts of the heart, emotion, and true self. I know you are thinking of things your little one can play with when you are not around; however, it is best to help him be creative by motivating him to create his own interim games. In many instances, the gift-giving is a sign of selfishness in that the caregiver really wants to gain more time to himself, and giving a toy is one way of rationalizing that fact.

Don't get me wrong, it is not always a matter of selfishness, and there is nothing wrong with being selfish, that's a gift of nature; however, **your** little "Bundle of Joy" needs **you** more than any toy. Even at Christmas time, when gifts are expected and appreciated, the advantage of **limiting** gifts and toys to just a few, and giving of **yourself** instead of a toy, is that in later life your Little One will better develop creative ways to entertain himself; in addition, **you** will be inclined to find more creative ways to entertain both him and yourself. The wonderful thing is, you don't have to be **extremely** creative, just do something. **Almost anything that comes from your heart will do just fine**.

"I'm bored, there is nothing to do!" Have you ever heard youngsters say that? Sure you have. That's the time he becomes more inclined to seek other avenues of joy, like drugs and entertainment from the dark side of our world. Reduce the number of toys, increase the creative effort from your heart and you will seldom, if ever, hear that weary phrase. Incidentally, toys are not bad: it's just that over-abundance of them is usually counter-productive. Again, a ball is a premier toy to place in your arsenal of tools to aid you and your Little One in his normal development.

One more thing: making toys from things around the house or out in the yard is another way of inducing creativity in yourself and your little one, that's important, and it is also economical. For example, find different size sticks in the yard and race them in water at a nearby creek (or even the bathtub), either one-on-one (mine and yours), or several (I'll take the short fat one, which one do you say will win?). It really doesn't matter who wins, but you'll find it fun and a learning adventure for both of you.

Now let's continue with launching your little "Bundle of Joy" on a lifetime of progress and success.

CHAPTER TWO

From Six Months to One Year

Change is a product of time, and he seems to change completely in his second six months of life. He sits up and turns over, plus he starts trying to talk in his own inimitable way. What really gets interesting is he tries to feed himself and seems to start to better understand what you are saying to him.

At this point, the most important thing is to encourage him in every way, especially point to the new skills he is acquiring. The best way to encourage him is with **praise**; he won't be perfect in anything he attempts, but he will make progress and that's when acknowledgement of his advances is paramount. He'll look to you and expect you to respond, that's when you can pick him up and tell him how wonderful he is, and remember to give him great big **hugs and kisses**.

A word of caution: this is the time he is extremely curious; he'll get into everything. With this in mind, you need to **childproof everything** in every room if possible. Everything that is **sharp** should be locked away. Anything that might **break or shatter** should be moved to "higher ground," or an area that is impervious to being pulled over. **Poisonous** items should be placed out of reach, and **electrical outlets** should be covered. All open **stairways** should be closed off or in some way childproofed.

She will want to place practically everything in her mouth, so **be very careful about what you leave laying around**. (That's a car key in Gervaise's mouth)

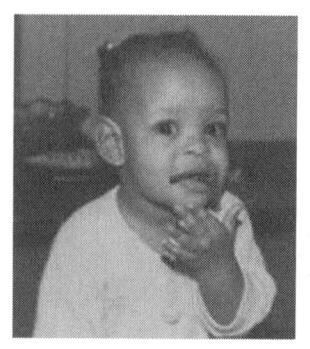

Let her explore as much as possible, and **try to limit the occasions for saying "no."** On the other hand, **do not shy away from saying "no" when appropriate (remember to develop and use PAPs)**: she might pout, but she'll get over it. When you say "no" there should be no hesitation on the actions of your Little One to change what she is doing immediately. Keep in mind, you should have a legitimate answer when she asks that soon-to-be-coming-question, "Why?" Incidentally, she is **born** secure and confident, and you want to do whatever it takes to support that trait.

When you are tempted to say no, remember the PAPs that you learned when we talked about the **three big things** and tough love. The older she gets, the more adept you will need to be when you put the PAPs on her. Your primary goal, however, is to guide her, you may not always grasp a good solid PAP. There are times when you will need to use the phrase, "Because I said so!" even though you know it is not a legitimate answer. Whenever that happens, try to recall the situation and give her a legitimate answer (or a smooth PAP) as soon as possible.

One important thing to remember: when you say "No," critique the behavior, not your Little One. For example, you could say, "You are a wonderful little girl and I love you very much, but you should never do that: and this is why" (always give a legitimate "why" in your own words).

To be more specific, let's say you observe your child knocking over a set of blocks another child is building, or has built. You could say, "I saw what you did, now I'm going to have to apologize to his parent(s). What do you think you should do?" Whatever his response, a review of the reason his behavior is inappropriate (not in his best interest) should be covered at the soonest appropriate moment. Enough said about that. You might say, "What would you do if a bigger, 'badder' child did the same to you (when I'm not with you)? Think about it!"

It is at this time that you want to encourage your Little One to "help" around the house. If you are peeling fruit, such as an apple or orange, give her one to look at and touch (and eat!)

If you are performing other activities, don't hesitate: encourage him to "help you" do other things as well. For example placing dishes in or taking them out of the tub, sink or dishwasher, sweeping the floor, running the vacuum cleaner, cutting grass, shoveling snow, and any normal activity. Also, try to provide clean, safe pans and utensils for pretend-cooking, or, as is probable, a coming together of the sounds of the kitchen (banging of the pans).

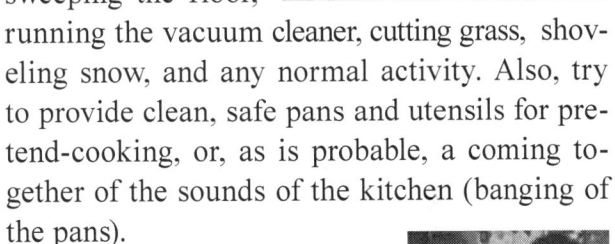

If you have not already begun, now is the time to **begin reading to your child – at least fifteen minutes each day**. Remember, for a child who has not yet learned to read, it is probably a strange, mysterious, yet fascinating process. **Reading is undoubtedly the single most important skill for him to master: mainly** because it is the key to all the other subjects he will learn: in school and in life. Plus, it is the key to worlds of pleasure and information via books, magazines, and newspapers.

Some parents might be embarrassed because they are either poor readers, or in some cases can't read at all. That doesn't matter. At whatever stage you reside, you are far ahead of your child, and you will continue to be ahead for quite a lengthy period of time. If nothing else, and if at no other time, now is the time you can **leave your legacy to the world – teach your child(ren) to read (even if you are in the process of teaching yourself)…**

The question is: when is he **ready** to read? The **technical** answer is, he is ready when he has the language skills, eye control, and emotional maturity needed to make a strong, steady effort. On the other hand, children begin maturing at different rates; therefore, there is no single age at which we can say your child **should** begin reading. The **real** answer is: he is ready when he is ready, but you may not know it unless you begin reading to him. On the other hand, you can speed the process and **motivate him** to **want** to read **by having fun** as you share the reading experience.

When you read to her, hold the book, or magazine at a level she can reach. If she starts grabbing for the pages, that's good, but show her how to turn them without soiling or tearing them. Look for stories with big print and lots of colorful pictures, and as you read the names of things and people in the books, ask her to name them and point to them in the pictures. Also, get her accustomed to reading the newspaper, that way you can keep her abreast of current events in the world around her. She won't know what you are talking about, but she'll grow into it and prosper in many ways.

Before we continue, allow me to share the internet address of an entrepreneur who has been very successful in teaching children to read. His name is Jim. He and his significant other, Alena, have developed a method that has proven to be very effective. If you have access to a computer,

From Six Months to One Year | 107

you might want to consider advancing to their site. You can access it by clicking here on my page titled, "Early World of Reading," or simply cut and paste to your address bar: http://www.childrenlearningreading.com/

To continue: One of the most valuable things you can do when out-and-about with him is to **ask questions**; for example, "Do you hear/see that?" Then describe the sounds and sights he hears/sees, and talk about what makes them; for example, train whistles (guess how many cars the locomotive is pulling!), thunder claps (how far away is the storm?), ambulance/police/fire sirens (which one is it: an ambulance, a fire truck, or police vehicle?), waterfall (of what does that sight/sound remind you?).

It is about this time that you want to begin teaching her about her body and how different parts relate to each other, plus their function (Andy Griffiths has written a delightful book titled, "What Body Part is That?" he must have had loads of fun writing it: you too can have loads of fun reading it); for example, the feet, where are they, and for what are they used. She will begin experimenting and exploring long before you are ready to talk about her body, but now is the time to begin the exploration with her.

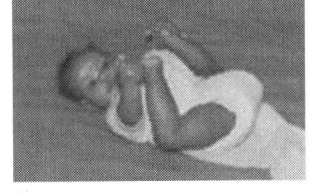

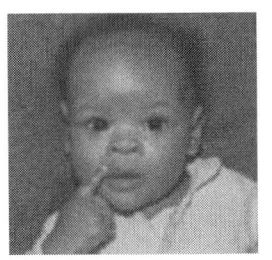

What is the mouth called, and for and what is it used, also how about the lips and the nose, the teeth and the tongue? How many eyes and ears does she have and why do people have only one mouth but two ears and two eyes. Some people say it means a person should see and hear twice as much as they speak. At this stage, she will be extremely curious, and now is an excellent time to take advantage of that extreme curiosity. A word of caution: don't overwhelm her with too many things at once, there will be plenty time for absorption. For example, point to her eyes and say, "What is this?" "Do you have more than one?" "What do you call the one to which you pointed?" "For what are they used?" "Tell me something you see that is red." "When you see red, of what does that remind you?"

You might want to make that day a special one. Call it the "eye day," and maybe once every year, on that day, go see something (the art museum, a dance, a movie, etc) in recognition of her special "eye day." You could do the same for the mouth. Make it the special "mouth day," and go eat something special on that special day: same thing for the ears, nose, lips, hair, etc (don't overdo it, the more you do, the less effective each one might become. No problem though, your instincts will guide you).

Also, you might want to consider having at least one special day each year in recognition of whatever turns her on the most, do something and make it special: nothing elaborate. Those special days could become reasons to celebrate being alive, achieve goals, and any number of things that tend to maintain the special bond between you and her.

One subtle point that might be added is that the same special day can only happen once a year. Let's see now: there are four quarters in the year, twelve months, but you don't want to do it too often because you want it to remain a special occasion. You could have a day in January for the ear day (go someplace to hear a special concert): April for a mouth day (special place to eat): July for an eye day (see a movie): October, a nose day (get her a bottle of perfume), etc.

When our older son, Logan, was in the second grade, his teacher thought he might have had Attention Deficit Disorder (ADD), so we took him to a testing center. They determined that he did not have ADD, he was simply a curious and healthy young boy. They determined two significant items though: they said his perception of numbers was extremely high (off the chart), and for his age he was extremely worldly. I attribute his worldliness to the fact that at the early stage, beginning at about six months, we would **show him new**

and different things. He was fascinated with construction equipment, so we spent a great deal of time **touring construction sites**.

We would look at cars up close and we'd point out the tires, the roof, the doors, the mirrors, and we'd identify their function. We would walk through new houses under construction (after hours) and talk about the structure and where would be the location of the bath, the basement, the bedrooms, kitchen, the garage, etc. We would **introduce him to different people that he was unaccustomed to seeing**, like the fuel deliveryman at the gas service station, the utility-meter reader in our neighborhood, etc. And to **new places** like the Laundromat, the shoe store, the post office.

We'd **sneak up on animals**; for example, a bird in its nest, and observe their actions and reactions.

We'd **ask questions and talk about what we saw**. All during this time, not only did Logan learn things, but I also learned new things that I didn't know myself. We had fun doing it, and we always found time to play together. We'd **play peek-a-boo and patty cake**, we'd **make silly faces** in the mirror; we'd **build towers and knock them down**. At the same time we would **insure that he knew that some kinds of behavior was not OK (the beginning of more formalized training to distinguish right and wrong)**. For example, knocking down the towers of other children, or biting, hitting, and throwing things except in games is **not OK**.

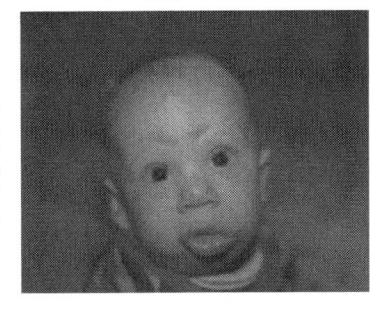

You should have no problem with saying no. Your child will seldom ask questions that are beyond your ability to answer; however, always have a ready and positive explanation for the "why-not." On the other hand, it's great when you don't have an answer because it provides a chance to gain another teaching moment, plus it offers the opportunity to guide him toward a means of getting correct answers when you are not around.

When you need to say "no," the instance can also provide a "teaching moment" about the value of money. We've stated a number of things about money: everything we've said about it is designed to openly mold his mind to the concept of it and where it fits in crafting his "Bridge to Success."

All this being said; at this stage in his existence, he has no idea about money, what it is, and why it might be important. However, remember what we said about him being unusually observant. If you have money problems, not only does he see it, he can sense it. If you are overly extravagant with money, that action de-values its significance. If you hoard money and treat it as though you will never have enough of it; that sends a message to him that he'd better be extremely frugal and protective of it because it may be taken away at the drop of a hat. An important fact about money is that in order for him to be well balanced about it, you need to have a joyful relationship with it yourself.

Remember what I said about money: you may think of it as something out in space, that it is separate from you; not so, money is the fruit of production and the essence of freedom. As long as you treat your actions around it as separate from who you really are, your Little One will probably (at best) have a slow start coalescing money with joy. That kind of puts a damper on that "barrel of fun" we talked about.

So as to not get off-topic here, I said it before, but maybe you missed it. Let me offer an idea that I think might be worth your consideration: talk with your Little One about something special that he (or you) wants to do or buy, place a monetary value on it: make it something that is small, within reach by the end of a month. If you don't have a "special holding place" make a big deal out of selecting one. At the end of each week, you and he place one fourth of the agreed upon sum in the "special holding place" (no big deal, but make it obvious). Then, at the end of the month, celebrate your achievement by doing, or buying what you planned to do or buy.

You don't need to do that a bunch of times to embed the concept within his mind, of living within his means, setting goals, planning to achieve them and celebrating the result.

Isn't life great? Sometimes, pretty simple too!

The secret is to do all the above with style and finesse; in other words, don't be extremely obvious, on the other, let it all hang out. Like we said about yes/no when referring to tough love, it's better to say we can wait to get it later (when we can afford it) than to say "Put it on the card."

This is also a grand time to help your little one **learn how things feel**. You might often climb trees and talk about the rough **tree bark** and compare it to the smoothness of the **petals of a flower**, the softness of **towels and blankets**, powdery **flour**, foamy **shaving cream**, and the coarseness of **sand and dirt**, also the wetness of **water**: describe what each one feels like.

When I was in phase-one with Logan and Troy, we would **walk in the rain** and **race sticks** in the **rushing water**; we would walk along the creek and race sticks in the creek too. We would **play in the mud** and get all grimy and mushy ("mom" didn't like the muddy clothes, but we had loads of fun).

In the wintertime we would **play in the snow**, and enjoy **snowball fights**.

Later, we would **talk about the fun we had and describe how it felt**. All those things were simple yet very personal and very effective means of guiding and directing our lives.

One thing that happened with my little girl, Gervaise, is that she did something that I knew she knew she should not have done (about nine months of age). I said to myself, "She's going hate me for it, but she's too young for me to expect her to reason it out, so I've got to spank her." I grabbed her little hand and spanked her on the back of it hard -- two times, and then hugged her and talked to her softly. As I looked in her eyes, explained why she had been spanked: she cried briefly, and then looked up at me as if to say, "Thanks, I needed that." I was blown away!

The point to be made here is that when you can look deep into your Little One's eyes and know she knows exactly what she is doing, it is time to start establishing and enforcing rules of behavior.

As we close out this first year, we might highlight one more thing: Worldbook Educational Products had a phenomenal program titled "Letter People." We would listen to the music and dance and sing along with the "letter people" as they sang. They no longer provide that program; however, the TV program "Sesame Street" provided something similar to it. It was fun for all of us, and it helped teach them rhythm, music, love and caring.

Incidentally, we can't do all things all the time, so **don't be afraid to ask for aid in helping your Little One**; I guarantee you, it's not a sign of weakness, but a sign of wisdom. **That first year is critical in forming a lifelong bond between you and her/him**, as well as the rest of her world. Regardless of what happens in the future, that first year is really something special. If you are seeking peace of mind and the joy and satisfaction of making a difference in your world, you can make it happen. The essential thing is to infuse discipline, blanket it with love, and endeavor to share the entire parent/child relationship as a matter of fun and progress.

Before we enter the next section, let me say one more thing. In spite of my success during stage one and two with my little ones; remember, there are five stages to parenting. Partial stage completion does not make a good/successful parent. One more thing: many parents try their very best to be a friend of their offspring; if friendship happens, that's great. However, your job is not to be your Little One's friend (that's "icing on the cake"); your job is to be a parent, a guide, a sculptor and confidante (that is one of the reasons, when possible, you want to talk a lot and share in the games they gravitate to the most).

Before we leave this most valuable first year, let's put in perspective the value of your Little One's self-esteem. High self-esteem comes from positive reflections around him; however, the external appearance does not insure inner peace. Oftentimes children who look sure and successful on the outside live behind a façade of phony confidence, alienation, neurotic defenses, and restless malcontent. In other words; inside, he feels inadequate regardless of how he appears on the outside.

The question I'm sure you are asking is, "How can a parent know what's going on inside his Little One?" The answer is, you can't; however, all is not lost, because all of us leave clues to the combination that might unlock the path to our insides: that includes your Little One. It could be, he grinds his teeth during sleeping (that could mean he's fighting inconsistency, there's something lacking in his self-esteem diet), it could be the character of his handwriting is inconsistent (the letters might be tiny, which might indicate he feels tiny and inadequate).

Nevertheless, all is not lost, that's the primary reason we said this book is a "problem prevention guide". The reason is because we have the value of the two essential ingredients: treat your child under the auspices of "**life is a barrel of fun**," and institute the **three big things**.

Ain't it a hoot! Your little one and the rest of us are counting on you. The wonderful thing is we know you can do it. Hug your Little One for us!

End of the first year!

SECTION TWO

THE FINAL FOUR

In part one of this joyful effort, we highlighted the fact that all things begin with thought, but nothing happens until we do something. That's why this book is a two-stage affair. An analogy might be that mental preparation of the parent is akin to a car's battery, the alternator, the generator; the action that he performs during the first few months is as the starter. The first year of the interaction between the caregiver and his Little One is undeniably the key to success and happiness of your new arrival.

The first year is undoubtedly the most influential year of a person's life. In that section, our guiding comments were intended to be simple and uncomplicated and I think they are. The same applies to this section, the only difference is that in this section you and your Little One are taken from the end of the first year to the end of year five – generally, right before she enters formal schooling. I call it "The Final Four."

However, let us not linger any longer; let's continue into the meat of this joyous undertaking.

Oh, (I almost forgot), at the beginning of year one you might consider establishing a "growing ritual;" what I mean by that is, at the beginning of each month, establish a "growth wall." On that wall, mark his height and weight increase/decrease. As usual, have fun with this "ritual" within his/her daily "barrel of fun." The action will provide a self-motivator for your Little One without pressure from outside him/herself. In other words, the growing ritual will probably motivate him to eat his spinach, or play games that require him to get off the couch, etc.

Isn't life exciting! It's a barrel of fun too; all you need to do is maintain control!

I want you to know, the following effort is <u>not</u> intended to be all-inclusive or in depth; however, it <u>is</u> intended to be very, very helpful and at the same time, simple and uncomplicated. Without further delay, let us fully partake of the essence of this joyful effort. We think you'll see your little "Bundle of Joy" a little differently and with eyes that light up with the joy of parenthood.

CHAPTER ONE

(From One to Two Years)

Think of all the fabulous things your little "Bundle of Joy" is going to learn this year: how to **walk** and **run**, and **how to be understood <u>for sure</u> that he is a real person**. He will make a tremendous leap during these twelve months, and you can help make the most of it.

When he was able to sit up, we talked about the premier toy that is probably the greatest aid in developing your child (of any tool in your arsenal): that's the ball. If you have not indulged your Little One before, now is the time to introduce the ball to its beginning use. In other words, teach him how to play "catch".

No need for me to reveal that playing "catch" involves two different activities: throwing and catching; however, with that in mind, I provide the blueprint for teaching your Little One to do both. That appears in Appendix E.

Making the most of it means, if you have not already begun, the beginning of this year is the time to introduce "**RAM Time**" – **R**ituals/ **R**ules **A**nd **M**orality guidance. A sense of right and wrong (morality) has to begin at home. It is at this time that your family, headed by you the parent(s), should plan a family code-of-conduct meeting so that at least three things can be set up ahead of time: <u>**rituals**</u>, <u>**rules of behavior**</u>, and <u>**consequences**</u> (if the rituals/rules are not followed, for any ill-behavior, the individual will pay a price to the rest of the family, not the police or courts).

It might be beneficial for you to review RAM Time (Chapter five), to renew the value of incorporating it in your family plans. We think it's extremely important; on the other hand, you're the boss!

Number one: Everything, without exception, begins in the mind. What we think about determines who we are, and who and what we will be. In other words, think positive and positive things will happen (key positive support-word: **SUCCESS**) -- in the same vein, if we think negative, negative things will tend to follow (key negative word to attack: **FEAR**). Even though fear can be a motivator, it is inconsistent with success. Keep in mind that if we do things that are right and proper, nothing can hurt us, therefore there is nothing to fear. However, it is crucial that our actions are consistent with our thoughts.

You might want to go back and review chapter three, "The Silent Spoiler."

Now back to your Little One.

Now that your Little One is more mobile, it's time to do another safety check. Make sure he can't open cabinets where medicine or household cleansers are stored. And by all means, put sharp or breakable objects out of reach. The goal, of course, is to eliminate the need for medical attention.

Because of his curiosity, he will get into a ton of things that will beg your patience. You can avoid having to say "no" all the time if you limit his opportunities for troublesome or dangerous behavior, and increase the choices of harmless activities. Make good use of soft and safe things; for example, cardboard boxes, ice cream containers, and diaper boxes can prove to be safe playful "toys."

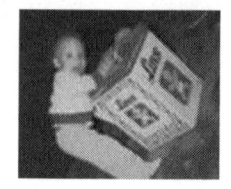

Give words to things he picks up and does; for example, "That's your rattle. Listen: it rattles when you shake it!" "Those are shoes: you place them on your feet so that your feet won't get hurt so easily."

Provide lots of praise; for example, say, "Good job" and "Thank you." "Way to go!" Encourage him with plenty of hugs and clapping, and smiles as well as words.

It is about this time that you want to begin encouraging him to say words for things instead of simply pointing to them. When he points to something, say, "What do you want to do, **ride the horsey** or **sit in the chair**?" Smile and say, "That's great!" when he tries to answer. Repeat the word as you answer his command. "Here's your **chair/ horsey!**"

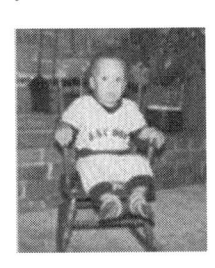

Usually, he is so hungry to find out what's going on in his new world that his eyes will follow your every move. Be sure to explain what you are doing some of the time, especially when you do something he has not seen before. For example, "I'm putting on my rain boots because it's raining outside and I don't want my feet to get wet." "It's cold outside, so I'm putting on my gloves so that my hands won't get too cold." However, it is important that you make it part of natural conversation, as opposed to an obvious lesson.

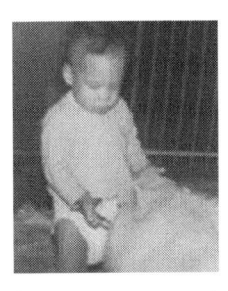

Introduce him to household pets like your dog or cat, and teach him to be gentle with animals as well as with other children. If you don't already own a pet, now is an excellent time to obtain one. Whether you have funds to buy one or not doesn't matters, because a person can always go to animal agencies where they would be delighted to provide a home for a pet at no charge. However, be sure to ask what you can expect your expenses to be once you adopt a pet, there is always some expense: be prepared.

Let him **see how things work**. Remember, practically everything is new to him. Show him how to **open a door** with a key, **zip a zipper**, **pour water**, and use a crayon.

Play direction games. Have him go **under** the table, **next** to the door, **inside** the bathroom, or **behind** a tree.

Take him to a playground. Talk about and show him how much fun children are having going **down** the slides, **back and forth** on the swings, and **up and down** on the teeter-totter.

Make a game out of learning the names of body parts. Have him wave his hands, **open** his mouth, **close** his eyes, and **wiggle** his toes (not all at the same time, just take it easy). Since hands and feet are so similar, you might want to do those on the same day! In fact, you might want to take the time to compare the thumb to the big toe, and name the fingers: the pinky, the pointer, the ring finger, etc.

Look for stories with pictures of animals, or better yet, plan a visit to a farm or petting-zoo. Have lots of fun with him by imitating the **sounds** the animals make. Some people may be embarrassed by doing this; however, when you are with your little one, that's the time, practically anything you do is okay. One of the caveats of being a parent is, you can be silly, it's the time to have outrageous fun – obviously, not every place is appropriate. Use discretion when warranted and teach him the truth in the adage that "**There is a time and place for everything**."

Insure that he understands that sometimes talking loud is inappropriate; in fact, sometimes talking at all is inappropriate; for example, in a house of worship, or during funeral services. Enjoying music is great, sometimes the louder the music the more entertaining it is. On the other hand, there are times that loud music is inappropriate; for example, in the wee small hours of the morning in an apartment building: you know the routine.

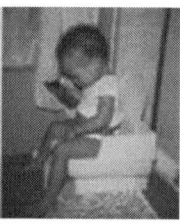

One more thing: during this year, your little one may not be close to being toilet trained yet – but don't worry about it. Keep in mind **patience** is very important, and **praise** is always much more effective than threats or punishment.

Now comes the "knight on the white horse," or whatever you call those individuals who have the answer to one or more of our illusive problems. Potty training is so much a matter of individual taste that, in my mind, there is an easy method designed just for you, but you'll never know it until you observe it from different outlooks.

I have found that the best way to find the potty training method perfectly suited for you is to access your favorite computer search engine (i.e. www.Yahoo.com, www.google.com, www.msn.com, etc.), search for "Potty Training Videos." Then scroll down to view any of the numerous videos that seem to be the answer for you: you'll find numerous techniques of which one is guaranteed to suit you best.

What a relief, now you can get on with your parent/child relationship in your own inimitable "barrel of fun."

Before we enter the next section, let me say one more thing. In spite of my success during stage one and two with Gervaise, Logan, and Troy; remember, there are five stages to parenting, partial stage completion does not necessarily make a good parent. One more thing, I just want to repeat: many parents try their very best to be a friend of their offspring; if friendship happens, that's great. However, your job is **not** to be your Little One's friend (that's "icing on the cake"); your job is to be a parent, a guide, a sculptor and confidante. I know, I've said that more than once before, but it's absolutely, positively extremely important.

Your Little One and the rest of us are counting on you. The wonderful thing is we know you can do it (we also know it'll help tremendously if you share this site with other parents).

CHAPTER TWO

From Two to Three Years

Your two-year-old is learning so much, so fast, that chances of her doing everything right is highly improbable. Try to keep your criticism low and your encouragement high. Learn how to use "time out" for inappropriate behavior; at the same time, tell and show her that you're proud of what she's learning. Incidentally, keep in mind that the use of "time out" should not be thought of as punishment, it is a method used to alter behavior. It is also a time that your Little One can improve the use of her imagination and creativity. Don't overdo it, but it can also be a time for **you** to re-group.

The library is one of your greatest sources of fun, entertainment, and association. On the other hand, if you can place it in your budget, and if you have not already done it, this might be the time to invest in a dictionary or a set of encyclopedias for your home. The primary reason is that when a "teaching moment" presents itself, you would be able to take advantage of that moment immediately.

This is a critical transition period for you and her because if you have kept pace with the guide of this book, she will tend to be ahead of her peers; that could be a good thing. On the other hand, if it causes her to be at the same position as her peers, that would be even better. However, that increases the challenge to keep her grounded while maintaining the "humilipride" of which we spoke. The goal during this period is twofold: first, you want to continue to teach, so that she continues to progress; at the same time, you want to integrate her behavior consistent with her age group. You do that by introducing yourself to parents of children in her age group, parents that you deem to have beliefs and tastes similar to yours. When appropriate, make a date with those parents and their children to share the joy of parenthood: visit parks, playgrounds, museums, movies, etc. alone (with your Little One) as well as with those other parents and their children. In later years, you and your child will have enhanced memories of friends and neighbors, even if you move away, sometimes especially if you move away.

Meanwhile, in the privacy of your one-on-one, give **names** to the things she looks at and plays with. For example, "Look how well you're stacking your **blocks**! Girl, that's great!" "Come ride on the **choo-choo train**." "That **doll house** sure is tiny; it's great how you keep it so clean and organized: I'm impressed!"

Talk about the **colors** she sees; for example, "Do you want to put on your **green** dress?" "Do you want to wear your **black** shoes or your **white** shoes?"

Talk about numbers: count out loud. Describe how you're putting on "one shoe, two shoes." Count the stairs as you climb them together.

Help your little one use words to express her feelings. Incidentally, if she tries to get her way by "throwing a temper tantrum," it is because you have lost control. The **<u>first time</u>** she attempts to manipulate you with that method is one of the times you need to respond with extreme kindness, disappointment, and total control. I know it's easier said than done; yet, you must immediately establish in her mind that inappropriate behavior is the best way to <u>not</u> get what she wants. It is important to note: how that translates into action does <u>not</u> depend on whether you are out-and-about or at home.

Let's be clear here: the most effective way to correct that errant behavior is to deny the option of doing what she wants to do. The situation is really a matter of control, therefore the most effective way to handle the potential problem is to adjust to the situation so that **<u>you</u>** are in control, not your child.

For example, "You're angry because you want to play with your doll, aren't you (identify the source of the errant behavior)? "No problem, you can do that later" (let her know that she can do what she wants to do);

however, her behavior makes that something she is not allowed to do at that time, "Right now, what else would you like to do?" (say it with a smile and undeniable control: project the fact that, because of her inappropriate behavior, doing what she wants to do is not an option at that time). The point is, you must stay calm, and totally in control. That's the most effective way to help adapt and regulate her behavior. Remember, a temper tantrum is not an optional behavior.

Make story time as much a part of the day as lunchtime. Get some toddler-level picture books from the library and include some rip-proof books with her playthings. Invite her to sit on your lap while you read a story or magazine, and comment on the articles and/or pictures.

Help her learn about time by talking about the daily schedule: "Grandma is coming over tonight for dinner, but first, its naptime."

When you are out-and-about together, talk about the things you **see** – a dandelion, a sea gull, a branch shaped like a "Y." Turn a walk into a chance to explore. Point out a tiny ant or a dark rain cloud.

Sit down together, close your eyes, and **listen**. Take turns describing what you **hear**. Hide a softly playing radio or musical toy in the room and have your Little One try to find it.

Help her learn about **sizes**. Gather big and small shoes, bowls, spoons, or boxes. Ask her to give you the small bowl or the big spoon, or to place the small shoe in the big box. Remember now, the most effective manner to get and keep her interested is to invent or design games for the things on which you want her to concentrate. For example, you could invent a "size game!" You make the rules: just off the top of my head, the rule could be that someone would be the "Size"—she would be the one who would select a part of the body that everyone else had to follow: eyes—I see something you don't see and it's red: what is it? Ears: I heard something that you might like and it's a sound, what sound is it? Nose: I smelled something that you might like, it's a food, what is it? Or something like that!

When your child can say her first name, teach her her full name -- first, middle, and last. Help her understand that she is a girl, that her brother (or cousin) is a boy, and explain the difference. By all means explain that bodies come in all **sizes**, **shapes**, and **colors** and that some are more appealing than others. Also, be sure to explain that a person does not choose her body, that it is simply a gift of nature, a wonderful container to store the real self. Be sure that you impress upon her that not all bodies are perfect, but that she should be thankful for hers, take care of it, and be proud of how it looks and performs.

If your Little One likes to group things together, cut out magazine pictures, and, together, place all the pictures of food in one stack, dolls in another, flowers in another. Ask her which doll or flower is her favorite, and why. Point out your favorite too, and tell her why. Later you can teach her to perform the cutting routine.

Finally, remember, the key to successful parenting is a blending of love and discipline; together they teach children how to deal with their world. The best way to discipline your Little One is with consistency and thoughtfulness, never with physical punishment or hurtful words. And always, when talking with her about misbehavior, address the behavior not who she is.

RAM Time is an excellent booster and support for everything related to behavior and communication with her; of course, the entire family is subject to RAM time. Use it wisely.

CHAPTER THREE

From Three to Four Years

This is the year of the "why." As tiresome as the endless questions might seem, remember that your Little One asks "why" because he wants to know how things relate to each other, and that's great. All "why questions" identify teaching moments: don't lose them. Answer his "whys" whenever you can, and when you can't (and sometimes, even when you can), just say, "That's a good question: let's find out." Then, as soon as possible, go to the source of the answer with him and look it up.

Incidentally, if he talks back, don't snap at him and don't interrupt, just listen intently, be patient and totally honest. Remember, it is a learning experience for both of you, and if approached properly, you will find that the success of your effort will be just as you visualize.

Help your three-year-old start learning self-help skills such as satisfying his toileting needs, **brushing his teeth**, washing his face and hands, and getting dressed and undressed. Start with the easier skills – taking off socks is a lot simpler than putting them on – praise his efforts sincerely and liberally, but don't overdo it.

Talk to him the way you'd talk to a friend; in other words, don't use baby talk: help him say words correctly. "Try to say water instead of wah-wah," but don't make a big deal out of it, it'll come. The important thing is to not make fun <u>of</u> him, have fun <u>with</u> him. However, on occasion, you also want to point out weaknesses in such a way that he acknowledges that he is fallible: have fun with it so that he will not have a problem laughing at and with himself.

Try to limit TV time to about one hour a day. Most children will have seen more than 4,000 hours of TV by the time they start kindergarten. You want him to do, not just watch. In other words, don't use the TV as a baby sitter.

Encourage him to help around the house. If he shows interest in setting the table, let him set out spoons or napkins for meals. If a spill needs to be cleaned up, show him where to find a towel. Show him how to put away some of his playthings and throw his dirty clothes in the laundry. Remember how Mr. Rogers would always hang up his sweater as soon as he entered the house? Of course, the reason is that the closet is where outerwear belongs when not being worn (not on the floor or on furniture).

Let him see how numbers are part of everyday life.

Help him count fruit at the grocery store, stamps for your bills and letters, or pennies for a treat.

Add a twist to story time: act out familiar stories and verses like "The Three Little Pigs," "Little Red Riding Hood," "Little Miss Moffat," and "The Cookie Monster." Use dolls or stuffed animals as characters, and give each a different voice.

Give him props to pretend with: old clothes to play "dress-up;" and clean, safe food containers to play "store."

Show him how to use his body in new ways: how to jump, hop, spin, and walk backward.

Make time for your Little One to play with others. That's the time your association with other parents becomes part of your teaching and allocating of time. Help him learn about sharing, taking turns, and other ways to cooperate.

Sing songs together, or leave out a word and let him finish: "Twinkle, twinkle, little _____." Try changing the words to songs or rhymes, and see if he can tell you what's wrong: for example, "Mary had a little pig, his tail was curly and white!"

Encourage his interests. If he likes cars, for example, check out car books from the library, and name the cars and trucks that pass by when you are out-and-about or in the car.

Let him explore art. If he enjoys scribbling and coloring, let him experiment with different kinds of paper, markers, crayons, or chalk.

Find time to just talk. Remember the first of our Big Three Things: talk a lot! According to one survey, parents talk to their children, on average, just a few minutes a day – usually giving orders. Talking with your child helps promote learning and love, it also aids the critical progress of self-discipline. Also remember, the more you talk with him at this stage, the easier it will be to accomplish. And, the easier it will be to talk with him later in life: when he is a teenager, for example.

CHAPTER FOUR

From Four to Five Years

Soon your little one will be starting kindergarten. By the first day of school, some children will have learned to ride a bike, others to tie their shoes. Some will be able to sink a basket with a basketball, others to do a cartwheel. Some will have learned to play a song on a guitar, others to help bake a cake. But no preschooler can or should be expected to do everything, or even keep up with his peers, so don't be concerned. Remember, he is special and his timetable is uniquely his.

Celebrate with your Little One for having her own special talents. Don't compare her to others, and try not to push her beyond her level of comfort. Try to say things that build her confidence, and avoid saying unkind things that can break her spirit.

Enjoy conversations with her – at the dinner table, at the grocery store, or in the car. Get her opinion on things; for example, what to cook for dinner or what errand to do first: ask her to give the reason for her decision. On the other hand, refrain from sounding like an interrogator.

Your little one can learn a lot when she's in the car with you. Talk with her about directions, signs and whatever else you happen to see.

After a read-aloud time or TV program, ask her to tell you about the story – what happened first, next, and last. Ask who her favorite characters were and why.

Help her learn to describe things, not just name them. Point out the "fast red convertible," not just the "car."

You may have an encyclopedia at home; that's great, nevertheless, visit the library regularly, and let your little one pick out books to read and enjoy. When you read together, try to get her to tell you what's happening by looking at the pictures.

Let her see you read for your own enjoyment – books, magazines, and newspapers.

Help her learn to recognize her own written name by printing it on her drawings or taping a name tag over her bed.

Teach her your "real" name. "You call me Daddy/Mommy, but my real name is _____."

Let her pick out the clothes she's going to wear each day. Give her choices – "Do you want to wear the blue dress or the red?" Be careful though: don't overwhelm her or yourself.

Teach her your family's phone number and address.

Look for community-sponsored children's activities like puppet shows and children's plays to attend together.

Prepare dinner together. If she likes to watch you cook, allow her to help you shell peas or snap beans.

Try to visit zoos and museums.

Turn on some concert, jazz, rhythm & blues, country & western, soul, and contemporary music, or borrow CDs from your library. Try to distinguish the different instruments – pianos, flutes, drums, guitars, trumpets, etc.

Together, practice counting groups of objects to ten. Count how many chairs, pillows, mirrors, or toothbrushes are in your house. Show your little one what the numbers look like.

Play school with your child. Turn the table on her now and then: allow her to take a turn as teacher.

If she asks a question you can't answer, that does not place you in a negative position. In fact, that becomes a sharing and teaching event, that's even better than a "teaching moment." Find the answer in an encyclopedia in the library. If your finances are such that you can purchase a set of encyclopedias for your home, by all means, do it. It will be one of the best investments you can make. Let her study the pictures while you read the details.

Make books together. Children like to tell stories. Write them down (in her words), and have her add the pictures.

Never leave your Little One home alone, no matter how briefly, and never have her watch other children. If your child has outside care, make sure you're welcome at any time. Have a clear understanding of the discipline they use.

CHAPTER FIVE

From Home to School

Remember, all children are different, even your twin is different from his brother. They develop at different times and in very different ways. Some children will enter school with more skills than others. Nevertheless, all children will work through kindergarten and the early grades to acquire learning skills along with your child.

Numbers and capacity interest children. Satisfy their curiosity with nursery rhymes, stories, and music. They will begin to count out loud (1 to 10 and beyond), understand empty and full, count objects like the three little pigs, "one, two, buckle my shoe…," etc.

Physical development is an important part of your little one's learning. He loves to move his body and use his hands. This is nature's way for children to develop different muscles. But youngsters start school at very different levels of physical development. In kindergarten children will join in activities that encourage running, jumping, hopping, skipping, and marching – throwing a ball – clapping hands – building with blocks – walking up and down stairs. They will also be using their hands to use crayons, markers, and pencils – cut and shape with scissors and paste objects – complete simple puzzles, fasten buttons and use zippers.

In addition to physical development, kindergarten teachers will be working with your Little One to develop social and emotional skills. They are perhaps the most important merging components children use and learn in their first classrooms. Teachers look forward to building on social skills that children know from home. They want to supplement your training, not initiate it: their goal is to help youngsters feel secure at school, and be confident working with others.

If you have kept up with us throughout this effort your Little One will enter school being able to integrate into the school culture and:
*feel good about himself
*be away from you without being upset
*take care of dressing himself and satisfying his toilet needs
*care for his own belongings such as coats, sweaters, boots, lunch, etc.
*understand basic safety rules
*complete planned activities
*follow simple classroom rules and routines
*know where he lives
*share his things with others
*plan and carry out activities with others
*work independently
*listen carefully
*be happy at school

When he enters the classroom, his world grows. It's natural for him to be a little anxious; and it's natural for you to be anxious as well. After all, both of you have a great deal of adjusting to do: first of all to being away from home, then to teachers, principals, and of course to other children. If you have followed along with me in this book and cherished and shared yourself with him, you and he will enjoy school together. It's a big beginning for both of you!

The major keys to the entire development of this new life, is just two things and they come in packages. First package: enjoy early learning with him and be sure he is read to frequently (at least fifteen minutes every day), encourage him to look at books and magazines, and be sure he is introduced to the library.

Even if you do nothing else, by all means be sure your little one is included in your family discussions. Package number two: "RAM Time" is the key ingredient in preparing him to expect and acquire a lifetime of success and happiness.

Be open, be real, and be the kind of parent he deserves. And by all means, be yourself and enjoy it; after all, there is no one else exactly like you. You only live once until you resurrect yourself via your offspring.

You can see how they progress outside via their personal appearance. However, there is much more to your child(ren) than their personal appearance, I'm referring to their psychological selves. For many, many years psychologist have focused on mental illness and its cure.

Studies show that the number of people who limp through life while suffering inner turmoil, and whose potentials are chained to neurotic hang-ups is staggering. Even though we regard our children as our most important and cherished national resource, parents are not trained to handle psychological problems of their child(ren).

This book does not attempt to train parents regarding handling inner concerns of their child(ren), it obviates it: that's why I titled it, "Bridge to Success: A **Parent's Problem Prevention Guide."**
The end: now, for a new/different beginning!

Bibliography

Title	Author(s)
Building Moral Intelligence	Michele Borba
How Good Parents Raise Great Kids	Alan Davidson & Robert Davidson
The New Dare To Discipline	Dr. James Dobson
Games To Play With Babies	Jackie Silberg
Your Child's Self Esteem	Dorothy Corkille Briggs
Playful Parents	Lawrence J. Cohen
God At The Kitchen Table	Scott Cooper
The Explosive Child	Ross W. Greene
Perfect Parenting: 1,000 Parenting Tips	Elizabeth Pantley
Discipline That Works	Dr. Thomas Gordon

Smart Discipline	Larry J. Koenig
The Preschool Years: Family Strategies That Work -- From Experts and Parents	Ellen Galinsky and Judy David
Setting Limits	Robert J. MacKenzie
Think And Grow Rich	Napoleon Hill
Perfectly Yourself: Lessons for Enduring Happiness	Matthew Kelly
The Intersection of Joy and Money	Mackey Miriam McNeill
Parenting the QBQ Way	John G. Miller (with Karen Miller)
What Body Part is That?	Andy Griffiths

APPENDIX C

Nursery Rhymes

In addition, a parent can attain incredible success by reading Mother Goose Nursery Rhymes to his little one. Many of the world's favorites are sprinkled throughout this book. The first line of each follows in alphabetical order:

Bye, bye black sheep have you any wool
Hey Diddle Diddle the cat and the fiddle
Hickory dickory dock, the mouse ran up the clock
Humpty Dumpty sat on a wall
Jack and Jill went up the hill to fetch a pail of water
Jack be nimble, Jack be quick
Jack Spratt could eat no fat
Little Boy Blue come blow your horn
Little Jack Horner sat in the corner
Little Miss Muffat sat on a tuffet
Mary had a little lamb
Mary, Mary, quite contrary
Old King Cole was a merry old soul
Old mother Hubbard went to the cupboard
One two, buckle my shoe, three, four, shut the door
Patty-cake, patty-cake bakers man
Peter Piper picked a peck of pickled peppers
Peter, Peter, pumpkin eater
Rain, rain go away come again another day
Ring around the rosey

Rock-a-bye baby on the tree top
Rub-a-dub dub, three men in a tub
Simple Simon met a pie man
Sing a song of sixpence
There was a crooked man who walked a crooked mile
There was an old woman who lived in a shoe
This little piggy went to the market, this little piggy stayed home
Three blind mice
Twinkle, twinkle little star

APPENDIX D*

Typical Course of Study (before computer input)

Kindergarten – Typical course of study (This is simply as a reference point)

Social Studies	Meanings of holidays, traditions, and customs Understanding and appreciating other cultures Individual's role in family, home, school, and community Relationship of the individual to	Work and jobs Safety rules and symbols Basic human needs Self-respect and self-awareness Awareness of others Locations of home and school Diagram of home and school the group
Science	Observation of everyday Familiar things Common animals and plants Interrelationships of animals and Classification of living things Farm animals Care of pets Like and unlike plants Indoor plants	The sun: our main source of energy source of energy Weather and seasons Light plants Colors Senses Earth, moon, stars, planets Simple measurement Beginning experimentations

Language Arts	Phonics Choral reading Listening to literature, music, poetry Nursery rhymes, fairy tales, fables Social listening Constructing visual images while Listening Roles play Oral communications skills Manuscript, handwriting	Following and giving directions Paraphrasing and summarizing Organizing ideas Experience stories Relating events and experiences Complete sentences Listening for correct speech habits and word usage Beginning writing process
Health and Safety	Personal hygiene Good eating habits Good grooming	Major body parts Physical fitness Safety to and from school
Mathematics	Simple counting to 20 One-to-one relationship Concepts of more, <, >, same as Sequence of events Correspondence of quantities Ordinal-cardinal relationship	Meaning of addition/ subtraction Introduction to number line Estimation Elementary geometry (shapes) Calendar and clock Denominations of money

Number-numeral relationship	Basic problem-solving strategies
Recognition of basic sets	Basic chart and graph concept

*From World Book, Inc ("Early World of Learning")

APPENDIX E

How to Control an Object

A few years ago, little boys were often asked, "What do you want to be when you grow up?" The answer usually was, "I don't know," or, "doctor," "lawyer," "fireman," etc. Seldom did they say, "I want to be a professional athlete!" A great deal of the time, that was what they were thinking. However, no one asked little girls that question. It was understood that when little girls grew up, they would be responsible for rearing the children, and assuring that everything relating to keeping the home suitable for maintaining a family, would be successful.

No need for me to agitate you, however, as I'm sure you are aware, in this, the twenty-first century, things have changed: many little girls have grown up to be doctors, lawyers, firemen, etc., and some of them have even become professional athletes. The point is, nature has provided little boys and little girls with different anatomical gifts; however, our society has discovered that, given the opportunity and equal preparation, little girls can do anything little boys can do in practically any activity selected.

Regardless of gender, one of the best things a little boy and girl can do is to engage in a competitive sport -- any sport. The marvelous thing about competitive sports is, the activity itself causes the participant to engage both the mind and body. Every day proves that males and females can perform incredible acts of strength, agility, and mental acumen under all kinds of conditions.

Professionals perform at much higher levels than most of us, and the marvel of their action is what keeps us eager to see them perform. Many people wonder how they can perform at such high levels. The answer is training and preparation; in other words, practice, practice, practice! However, we are not talking about professional athletes; as you know, we are talking about your little "Bundle of Joy."

You may say (or think) "He is just experiencing the joy of controlling his body, aren't we a bit premature in talking about objects outside of himself? "I say, "Probably, but not necessarily! "All I say is, don't assume he can/cannot perform physical acts involving the body; on the other hand, you have plenty time to be prepared when he is ready, but don't push anything on him. Just allow his actions to guide you: keep in mind just because you were a good/great athlete means only that he will be inclined to be athletically talented -- but not necessarily. I repeat: **allow his actions to guide you**.

On the other hand, maybe you are not athletically inclined, but guess what? That's great -- if you're not athletically inclined, you are ahead of parents who are. You might say, "This guy must be some kind of nut, how can that be?" Well, you might be right about me being "some kind of nut," (your words not mine), but, be that as it may, before you can teach your Little One some things, you've got to teach yourself.

Keep in mind, we're not talking about anything intricate, nothing complicated; we're just talking about elemental things that you already know how to do. Now, you'll be looking at these elemental activities from a teaching standpoint, as well as a learning standpoint. Teaching, because that activity alone will cause you to interact and bond with your Little One. Learning: because his performance will allow you to determine if he is inclined to excel in activities that require greater expertise with the upper, lower, or neither part of his body. Keep in mind, even if his athleticism appears to be negligible, his "Smile Index" (SI) will guide you to the stopping point.

You'll probably want to improve your ability to do the things that you'll be teaching your Little One, that's normal. The thing you want to do, beyond anything else though, is make it fun. How does one do that?

The method is a four-step technique and mindset: (1) Focus on one activity at a time (let your child's Smile Index (SI) determine the end of the teaching session, (2) errors will be encountered every step of the way, either by teaching-technique or application; however, never be afraid to laugh **at yourself** and/or **with others** -- sometimes you may look foolish, but be open about it, not too serious**,** (3) remember, practice erases errors, so, practice, practice, practice, but not to the point where it erases the fun of parenting, (4) progress encourages celebration: your Little One will not master anything the first time around, but as soon as he shows progress, that's when the hugs and kisses should be unleashed (don't overdo it you clown -- you called me a nut so I... Oh yeah, that was sort of a supposition on my part wasn't it?), all I can say is, "if the shoe fits, wear it".

Incidentally, once the practice has been completed for that session, it's Miller time (no, no, you idiot, it's soda, ice cream, hot dog, etc.) time. Oh, sorry about that, I just get carried away sometime!

Now that we have forged ahead into the realm of parent's mindset, let's move to the action part -- Throwing, Catching, kicking, etc...(it's about time... I know, I know, I'm an idiot!... Your words not mine).

How to Throw a Ball (any object)

In case you came straight here before reading the earlier portion of this work, I want to recap what we said before, to kind of warm you up.

A few years ago, little boys were often asked, "What do you want to be when you grow up?" The answer usually was, "I don't know," or, doctor, lawyer, fireman, etc. Seldom did they say, "I want to be a professional athlete!" A great deal of the time that was what they were thinking; however, no one asked little girls that question. It was understood that when little girls grew up, they would be responsible for rearing the children, and assuring that everything relating to keeping the home suitable for maintaining a family would be successful.

In this, the twenty-first century, things have changed: many little girls have grown up to be doctors, lawyers, firemen, etc., and some of them have become professional athletes. The point is, nature has provided little boys and little girls with different anatomical gifts; however, our society has discovered that, given the opportunity and equal preparation, little girls can do anything little boys can do in practically any activity selected.

One of the best things a little boy and girl can do is engage in a competitive sport -- any sport. The marvelous thing about competitive sports is that every day it is proven that people can perform incredible acts of strength, agility, and mentality under all kinds of conditions. Professionals perform at much higher levels than most of us, and the marvel of their performance is what keeps us eager to watch them.

Many people wonder how they can perform at such high levels. The answer is training and preparation (practice, practice, practice).

To continue: Every physical sport uses the entire body to perform at high levels, and practically all of them begin with the art of throwing and catching. With that in mind, the first thing we will do is teach the art of throwing a ball. The main reason is, an individual doesn't need anyone else to perform his magic, your Little One can practice all by himself, and enjoy it!

It probably seems obvious, but throwing a ball, requires the person to first hold on to it. If the object is small enough to be held in the palm of the hand facing the ground, as in baseball or softball, holding it can be done with one hand. We call this "the grip."

The proper way to grip a ball is to place the forefinger and the middle finger on top of the ball: the thumb on one side, and the ring and little finger on the opposite side.

Once the grip has been fixed, the first thing a person must do is to visualize a line that cuts the body at the waist into an upper and lower part. We call this the "H" (horizontal) line or the **"belt line"**. This line goes from left to right. Hence, there is an upper and lower. The head, arms, shoulders, and hands are part of the upper: the waist, legs, knees, and feet are part of the lower.

An example of the "H" line at work is: while bending your knees, try to touch your toes with your fingers. No need to strain: do it a few fun-times (easy, huh?).

Next, visualize a line that cuts the body into side-by-side halves. We call this the "V" (vertical) line or the **"zipper line"**: it goes up and down. The left shoulder, arm, elbow, hand, and hip along with the left leg, knee, and foot are part of the left half. The same parts of the body on the other side are called the right half.

An example of the "V" line at work is: stand facing a person or any object (like a tree). While bending your knees, try to turn your left shoulder so that it follows your left wrist as it tries to touch your right knee. Do the same thing with your right shoulder and right wrist (this time, touch your left knee). Again, no need to strain: just do it a few fun-times.

The goal is to work toward getting all parts of the body working together, smoothly as if they are one.

The difference between throwing and slinging is that generally to throw an object, as in baseball and football, it must be released from above the shoulder. To sling an object, as in softball and bowling, it must be released from a position below the shoulder (generally below the waist).

To throw with precision and accuracy, stand facing a person or object. Fix the eyes on the exact spot you want the object to strike. The spot is called the target. Raise the hands in front at waist high, bend the knees comfortably, and adjust the weight of your body to rest on the balls of both feet equally: the feet should be about shoulder width apart. This is called the starting position.

The following steps will apply for each and every throw and/or sling:

Step one: stand erect, feet about shoulder width apart hold the object you intend to throw (ball, stick, rock) firmly in front of you with both hands touching it.

Step two: stare at the exact spot you intend to hit, again, that spot is called the target.

Step three: to **throw**, use one hand to push the object up and over the shoulder in which the ball is being held, (as in baseball and football).

To **sling**, push straight back at knee level or below, as in softball and bowling.

(Remember to hold the object firmly, but do not squeeze).

Stop at this point: Practice over and over until this step is completed smoothly.

Step four: step toward the target with the foot opposite the hand in which the ball is being held.

Step five: move the shoulder, the hand, and arm in which the ball is being held, in the opposite direction and as far away from the target as possible.

At the same time, move the other shoulder in the direction of the target (Remember the "V" line at work)

Step six: bend the same knee in which the ball is being held, push the upper body toward the target.

Step seven: at the same time, fling the ball toward the target – important: the arm and hand will continue to move toward the target, that's good, it promotes accuracy and precision – it's called the follow-through, it should be emphasized with each throw.

Step eight: Bring the foot, leg, arm and hand that held the ball, alongside the other foot. (You should now be in the starting position)

This completes the lesson on **how to throw** (or sling) a ball (any object).

How to catch a ball (any object)

One of the most magical, simple, and fun games of all time is to play "catch". Children of all ages can participate with friends, relatives, neighbors and parents. The game is almost guaranteed to provide a simple and sometimes electric means of bonding with your Little One.

Obviously, there are two phases to the game of "catch": throwing and catching. We've already taken care of throwing: it's a little simpler because your child can have complete control of when, where, and under what conditions he participates. In addition, for him, it can be completely safe.

To catch an object, conditions can be a little more hazardous. However, you can establish a safe way of preparing a totally controlled means of practicing "catch" as well. The way to do that is to find a suitable wall, accompanied by a flat ground or floor. Then your child can practice both throwing and catching under conditions that he can control.

In addition to the above, you can set your sites on the satisfaction of knowing that playing "catch" is one of the simplest and safest methods of eliminating the phrase, "I'm bored, there is nothing to do!" Simply stated, your child must know how to catch an object: that's where you enter the picture. The following is your blueprint of teaching "how to play the game of 'catch.'"

I'm aware you are raring to go, so let's start!

Before we really get going (I know, I know, another interruption: I just want to insure we are at the proper starting point), let's re-establish the understanding of the body's integrated function during the act of throwing and/or catching.

Once the grip has been fixed, the first thing you teach him is to visualize a line that cuts the body at the waist into an upper and lower part. We call this the "H" (horizontal) line or the "**belt line**". This line goes from left to right. Hence, there is an upper part and lower. The head, arms, shoulders, and hands comprise the upper: the waist, legs, knees, and feet comprise the lower.

Next, visualize a line that cuts the body into side by-side halves. We call this the "V" (vertical) line or the "**zipper line**": it goes up and down. The left shoulder, arm, elbow, hand, and hip along with the left leg, knee, and foot comprise the left half. The same parts of the body on the other side comprises the right half.

The goal is to work toward getting all body parts working together, smoothly as if they are one. If he has not achieved that goal, work on it every day until he becomes proficient at it. Remember, he doesn't have to be proficient, all you're looking for is progress (just a tiny bit is adequate): keep in mind, the primary goal is to have fun. His "smile index" (SI) is the clue.

Before you get carried away with anticipation of having tons of fun with your child, plan to go slowly, be patient and make it little mini segments of fun-activity. The idea is to be careful with your Little One **before** it becomes a chore and before he gets injured: the reason is, he can easily be injured (injuries is one way the "silent spoiler" can infiltrate your progress). Incidentally, injury is of minimal importance because recovering from injuries is part of progress: it is also part of strengthening your child's inner resolve to be the best he can be. At any rate, in an effort to reduce the chances of injury, use three phases to teach catching.

Phase one: a ball rolling on the ground. Phase two: a ball above the head, commonly referred to as a fly ball. Phase three: an object headed straight toward your Little One: he has to either catch it or get out of the way (that's why it could be a safety hazard).

Keys to success:

1) As you release the ball in phase one, two, and three: use a <u>slinging</u> (underhand) motion.

2) As soon as the ball leaves your hand, teach him to, as quickly as possible, place the "V-line" ("zipper") directly in front of the ball.
3) Teach him to always keep his eyes on the ball, and always attempt to use both hands (that tends to promote greater balance and quickness).

Before continuing: practice the "belt line"/ "zipper line" combo at work. Don't complicate it, if you use the step by step approach, you and your child will appreciate the simplicity, ease and effectiveness of it. Here's the step by step:

Step #1: stand with feet shoulder width apart. Step #2: bend your knees, at the same time rest your hands on your knees (these two steps are very simple, but oh so important, we call this combo the "starting position," it establishes balance and facilitates quickness). Step3: touch your right toe with your left mid finger, return to the starting position. Step #4: touch your left toe with your right mid finger, return to the starting position. Step #5: touch the ground three times with both mid fingers touching each other, return to starting position.

Do this a few fun-times without stopping.

Phase one: a rolling ball. Listen to the rustle of the leaves and rocks as the ball rolls over and around them. Teach him to:

1) Have his feet spread about shoulder width apart.
2) bend his knees and lower his shoulders (#1 and 2 is the starting position).
3) position the weight of his body on the balls of both feet evenly.
4) place both hands side-by-side with the palms facing the source (your hand)
5) as the ball rolls toward him, make sure the fingertips of both hands touch the ground.

He probably won't get it right, right away, but as he progresses, acknowledge it and praise him (you might have an urge, for sure you want to praise him, but don't overdo it; On the other hand, when he executes it perfectly, that's when you let it all hang out (watch him glow!).

At the end of the session, be sure to take a refreshing break: soda, ice cream, hot dog (whatever he has a hankering for).

<u>Phase two</u>: fly balls. This is when the ball is looped above his head. Teach him step one is always the starting position. In addition, the palms of his hands should always face the ball.

In all phases instruct him to place his hands directly in the path of the ball so as to stop its movement; in other words, prevent the ball from getting past him.

<u>Important</u>: if the ball is below the waist, catch it with the fingers pointing toward the ground. If above the shoulders, the fingers should be pointing toward the sky.

After he has become proficient with phase one and two, it is time for you to begin teaching direct-line catches. Move closer to him (five yards or less). As he or she becomes more proficient, little by little (unless he asks, not during the same day), continue to increase the distance between the two of you. In other words, if it's five yards today, and he has made no or negligible progress, make it five yards tomorrow; on the other hand, if he is improving rapidly, you might want to make it six to ten yards the following day. You be the judge, of course you are always in control; nevertheless, when it comes to any kind of game, never shy away from, in fact, promote his participation in decision-making.

As soon as the ball touches the hands, teach him to grab the ball and position the body into the starting position: immediately preparing to throw it back to the source (your hands).

Suggestion: unless he requests otherwise, during any one session, teach only phase one, phase two, or phase three. On the other hand, if he is rapidly proficient in one or more phases, there is no need for you to shy away from combinations. You are in complete control, which means it's your decision.

One more thing, at the advanced stage, you might want to begin <u>throwing</u> the ball (as opposed to slinging it: you'll know when to make the adjustment).

That completes the lesson on how to catch a ball: if you have already completed the lesson, "how to throw an object," you are now ready to teach him the fun of playing "catch." And you, our parenting hero, are ready to continue to observe your Little One develop into a tower of power. In addition, you now have an additional tool to assist you in the process of bonding with him/her.

Before we leave this area, let's talk about variations of of this great bonding tool

Games (Variations) (Physical/Mental)

Life in the "Barrel of fun" of which we speak is really something special! All children will excel in certain aspects of identifying who they are. Becoming adept at directing your Little One to participate in a wide variety of games is the easiest way to identify what turns him on. When it comes to games, some children will excel physically: you'll be able to identify in which variation your Little One fits by using the foundation of discovery. What I mean by that is if he excels physically use the game of "catch" to advance to another level of activity.

For example, if he excels by bouncing the ball with his hands, you might want to introduce basketball: teach him to first bounce the ball, then shoot, etc. If he excels with his feet, introduce soccer and all the trappings that involve using the feet, etc. One of the keys is don't take him too fast, allow him to lead you, just be observant and take physical and/or mental notes. The next level would be to teach him how to excel at defeating an obstruction, if that's true, you might want to introduce tennis, volleyball, badminton, bowling, etc.

By the way, just because he might not appear to be as gifted as you are physically, he may still approach the love of your sport from the aspect of coaching or managing. Again, don't force it, but don't rule it out.

On the other hand, maybe the physical does not float his boat; no problem, if he is more mental than physical, reading is the foundation to explore his mental acumen. If he excels in reading, he might get turned on by rhyming words, maybe he'll be a poet, a songwriter or musician, or simply a writer (like me or you, his hero), etc. Or maybe he is intrigued by the rhythm of playing checkers, then maybe advance to chess. Don't forget about photography, drawing, playing cards, magic acts. There is practically no end to the things you and your Little One can access in an attempt to identify his hot button.

One of the keys to your success is don't force him, simply introduce a wide variety of games, let his **smile index** lead you to the engine that drives his "barrel of fun". By the way, don't forget games such as roller/ice skating, hockey, gymnastics, curling, archery, skiing, swimming, equestrian, and on and on.

All the time during the interaction with your Little One, keep in mind, you want to mold a balanced child. In other words, don't avoid either the physical or mental. The result is, he will be at home regardless of his environment (among friends and foe alike).

You'll find that as you pursue the nature of the contents of his "barrel of fun," your Little One will enter the world of progress at an ever increasing rate of growth. You will be the catalyst that starts that engine.

Are you as excited about your prospects of molding your little stick of dynamite as I am? You should be. The world will be his to hold, you will be the sculptor!

I think you'll admit: that's exciting! (If not, maybe I'm just a fuddy duddy, but I'm excited **for** you!)

Oh to be a parent again! There is no greater endeavor in the whole wide world than parenthood. Remember, you hold the key to unlocking the joy of living inside the "Barrel of Fun" with your Little One. Enjoy it, it's a once in a lifetime trip to immortality.

Isn't life a barrel of fun! All I can say is, make the most of it (life)!

Remember back in chapter one, I said, "In addition to my Grandpa and grandma, there are five parents and their spouses whom I'd like to acknowledge because they have proven the value of good/successful parenting," remember that? The next section is where I acknowledge those extra special individuals.

APPENDIX F

Acknowledgement

This work is dedicated to an incredible man I heard about but never knew: he was more than just a parent, he was an inspiration to all who knew him. His name is Noah Williamson: he is pictured here with my grandma and most of their offspring: the other individuals in the vehicle are some of my aunts and uncles. Inspiration is an understatement for my amazing grandpa, you'll understand why I say that when you read about him (and others) in this section.

164 | Part Two: Section Two

Each of the above Americans faced racism, discrimination, and legalized segregation in the South. However, with determination and drive all of them forged ahead to make conditions suitable to serve their desires and needs. Unlike many black Americans, they did not think of themselves as victims.

The "Local Voices" article of July 4, 2001 relates to this picture in a big way.

Fifty Years Later

Acknowledgement | 165

This work is also dedicated to the clean and innocent individuals all over the world personified by my offspring Logan, Gervaise, and Troy: the refreshing innocence of youth causes an inside warmness that generates joy...

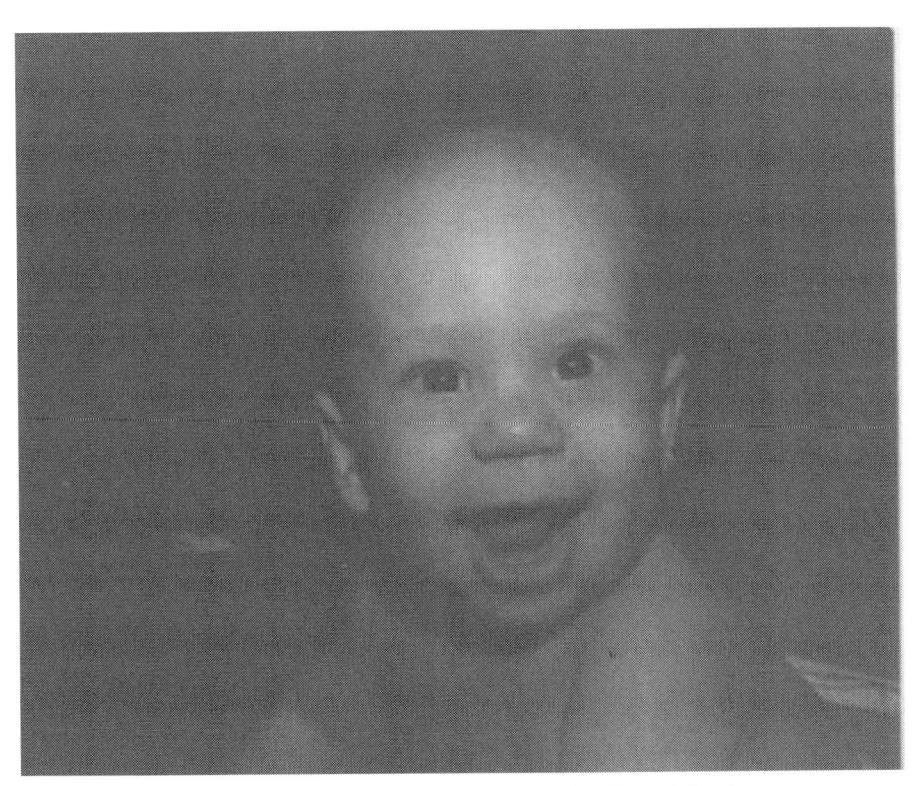

This was my son Logan: October 1980. Revel in the pure innocence of that grin.

This is the picture of that proud young man as a graduate from High School

Acknowledgement | 167

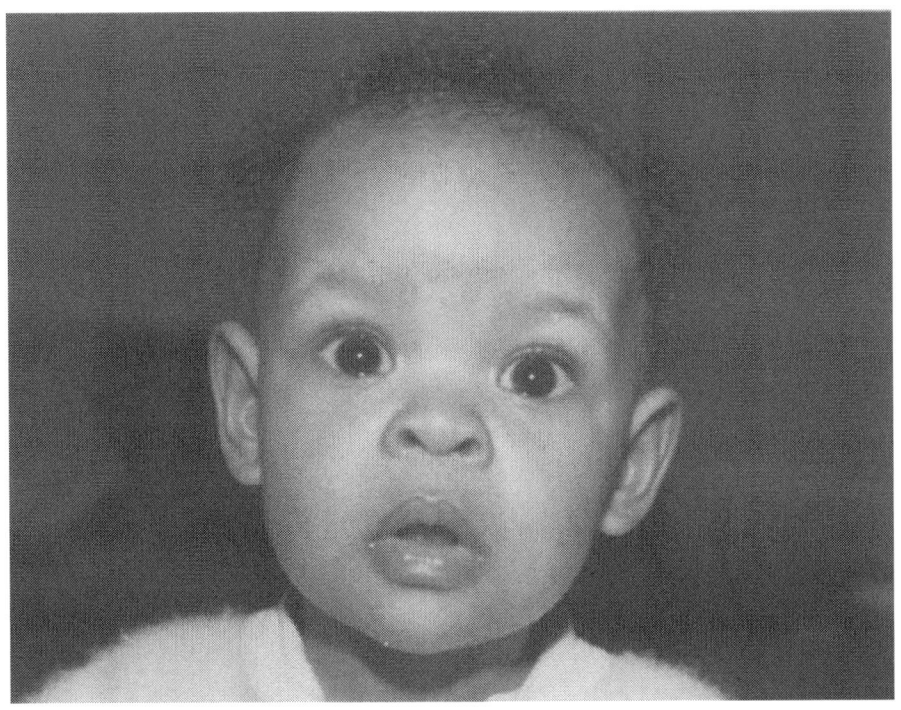

This was my daughter, Gervaise, July 1971. The essence of innocence.

Here she is as a High School graduate

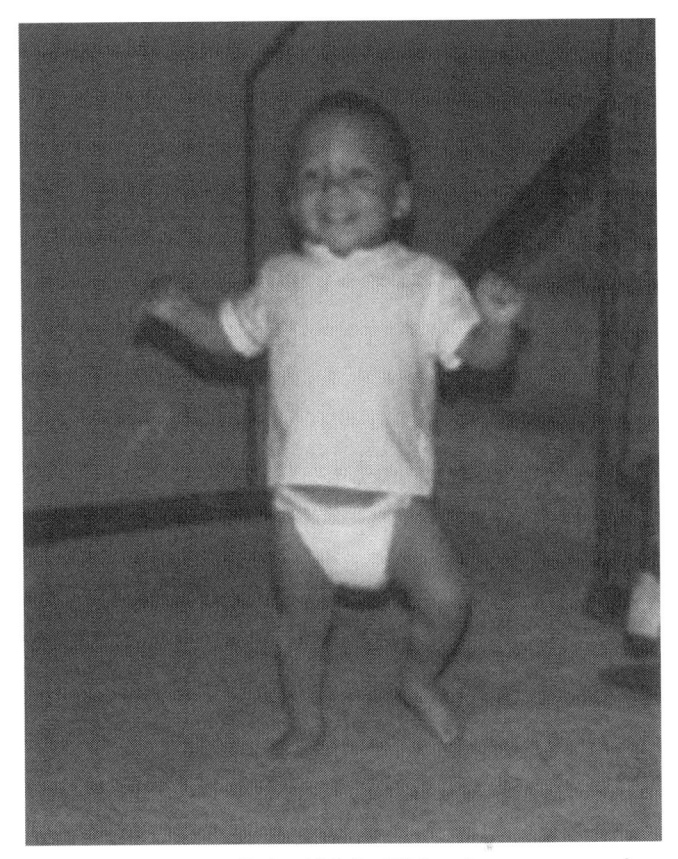

This was my son Troy (July 1984). This picture was taken when we lived in a tri-level home: this was the first day he took multiple steps unattended. He walked about ten steps to his mom, Bonnie – she hugged and praised him, he immediately crawled back to the steps you see behind him here, raised himself and proceeded to walk (almost run) to Bonnie about four or five different times. What an eventful day, we also have it on tape!

Unfortunately, we cannot maintain that pure innocence, change will not allow it; however, we can mold our little "Bundle of Joy" to become the most powerful and creative self our Creator intended him to be.

170 | Part Two: Section Two

Here he is again graduating with Honors!

Many individuals are responsible for the success of this work; however, I'd like to briefly acknowledge five parent-couples who have proven the adage, "The proof of the pudding is in the eating." The parents I highlight here have taught their offspring to be independent and at the same time, promote and accentuate the value of belief in a power that binds our spiritual self to the real world.

The first is Darryl & Tracy. They have molded and guided their son and daughter to understand the challenges of life: both of their children are headed for independent and responsible adulthood. Tracy is a school teacher: Darryl is a gifted businessman, athlete, basketball/football coach, and pastor of a church in Cincinnati, Ohio. If I were asked to name one parent, above all the others it has been my pleasure with whom I have been associated, he would be the one.

Next is Keith & Glenda have guided and molded three college graduates, plus their youngest is an incredibly gifted and insightful pre-teen. In addition, they opened their hearts and home by adopting a young male and female into their family environment. They join me in being grandparents for the first time. Glenda is a homemaker and Teacher's Aid. Keith is a chemist, a results-oriented leader for a major international corporation, and is hands-on involved with his church.

There is no order here, it's just that each of these parents have proven the success outlined in our "Bridge to Success".

Next is Wayne and Becky, they are extraordinary individuals in their own right and as a couple they are a dynamic duo. Becky is a social worker, now working with the legal profession in her community. Wayne is a retired chemist; and is now a substitute teacher for his local school system. A few years ago one of their boys qualified for, and was accepted at the Air Force Academy: he is now a colonel in the Air Force and teaches other officers the art of aerodynamics. Another of his sons is practicing in the ministry. One of his daughters is a nurse, another is Director of a major horticulture center, still another was working fulltime and simultaneously attending college fulltime, has now graduated with honors and has found and married her soul mate.

A few years ago, both Wayne & Becky were volunteer ministers in a program in their community for youth gone astray (sponsored by the court system in their county). The astonishing part of their involvement with the courts back then is, none of their off-spring was involved with the legal system in any way.

Sometimes, for various reasons, a parent and child may be stripped apart. Not a problem with Lenny and Amy. They became accustomed to traveling several hundred miles each month in support of his daughter, a multi-talented dancer and beauty queen. Amy is a psychotherapist and Lenny is a real estate and stock market investor. Together they had not only insured that his parents were properly cared for in their twilight years, they also insured that his daughter was properly grounded mentally and physically, and will never ever have financial or adverse mental concerns.

I'll never forget the day Bonnie and I were working in our back yard when a young couple looked over our back fence and introduced themselves. He was a school teacher and she a homemaker, they both were local missionaries for their church. Charlie and Susan were and are heavy-duty believers in the word of God.

Since then they increased their family by five-fold: Susan has maintained the role of homemaker and Charlie advanced from school teacher to law school, to lawyer, to judge. I must say of all the individuals I have known in more than seven decades of life, Charlie is probably the most impressive individual of all. He lives his life in the uncompromising path leading from the purity and goodness of the soul.

The wonderful thing about the above couples is not what they have gotten out of life; it is what they have given to others to make life worth living. Their off-spring are living proof of the value of good/successful parenting: society is strengthened by the results of their tender offering. They are outstanding, and worthy of tributes to their achievement.

Having said that, I want to acknowledge one more set of people: my family. If you will recall, in the opening frame, I dedicated this work to my grandpa. I said he was an incredible man and an inspiration to all who knew him. Well, let me tell you about my grandpa Noah. Before I was even thought of, with his sweetheart, Bertha, he had fathered six children when disaster struck. He was run over by a railroad train. Though his life was spared, he lost both legs – a little bit above the knees. That's why he was not behind the wheel of the car in the picture shown at the initial acknowledgement of this work.

Not only did he survive that traumatic event, he remained active and fathered the remaining offspring you see in the picture. There is more to being an inspiration than just surviving the catastrophic event that he experienced: he was an unusually effective parent.

Not only was he a black man in the heart of the South, he was a business owner, a homeowner, and more. Each of my uncles and aunts left an indelible mark on society: my dad was a master mechanic, plus he owned one of the largest garages on the south side of Chicago. The garage was large enough to house upwards of 175 cars, and included mechanics, fueling and cleaning facilities, and he built (from the ground up) sixteen tow trucks.

One of my uncles owned a bank. At the same time he was a powerful councilman in Atlanta, Georgia. When I was a youngster, he was not one of my favorite uncles because he wouldn't give me anything unless I did something to earn it. Nevertheless, not only was he a shrewd and powerful banker and politician, practically all who knew him, including me, appreciated and loved him. Three of my aunts were teachers and administrators in the school systems in Atlanta, Georgia and Detroit, Michigan. One of my uncles was a baker and owned a bakery, another owned a restaurant.

I could continue because there is more; however, there is no need. The point is, my grandpa Noah and "Big Mama" Bertha, were incredible parents and an inspiration to all who knew them.

Finally, I want to acknowledge one more set of people: my immediate offspring, the most seasoned is my daughter, Gervaise. She has provided me with the distinguished title of grandparent, she is still "my little lady," and a fine daughter and mother of Monet. My sons, Logan and Troy, are powerful young men who have overcome obstacles that lesser men would not have survived. I am so proud of them that I could shout. Then there is Bonnie, my partner and wife. Many people dream about what they can do to help their family members, Bonnie actually lives the dream. In addition, she thinks not just what she can do to help family members, she includes friends and neighbors as well -- she is an amazing woman! I won't even mention how she managed to survive life with me and my unusual decisions (to say the least).

Now that we have come to the end of this work, I just want to say, I sure am pleased that you chose to share a little of your precious time with me. One more thing, just one (I promise): don't be a "lousy parent," – touch a lot, hug a lot, communicate a lot, and above all be a disciplinarian with love.

This is the End of this Parenting package.

One more time:

Hug a lot, Love a lot, and Lot's of PAP's. Above all remember, pursuing Discipline with passion enveloped with a blanket of Love, is the foundation of parenting success.

Meanwhile,

Make it happen and make it fun!

Made in the USA
Charleston, SC
08 October 2014